The Overstuffed Book of

Armchair Puzzlers™

Sink Back and Solve Away!™

Stuffed Full of Fun!

CROSSWORDS ✶ WORD PUZZLES
WORD SEARCHES ✶ CRYPTOGRAMS

UNIVERSITY GAMES

The Overstuffed Book of
Armchair Puzzlers
Sink Back and Solve Away!™

Editorial Director: Erin Conley

Designer: Lisa Yordy

Special thanks to the entire UG pinch-hitting proofing team
led by Suzanne Cracraft!

ISBN 1-57528-928-8

Table of Contents

3

Introduction

Welcome to the world of *Armchair Puzzlers*. If this is your first time trying an *Armchair Puzzler* book, we are thrilled to have you join us. If you are a veteran reader of our books, we are sure that you will be challenged and entertained. This book is the ninth in the series and the first to combine the work of more than one author, containing multiple types of puzzles written by three different puzzle masters.

The *Armchair Puzzlers* series started in 2003 when our editor Erin Conley and I asked several of our top game inventors to share their favorite puzzles and create new ones for this exciting book series. Jeff reached back to his college days at Stanford and put together a fun book of crosswords. Maria injected humor and wit into the normally stuffy fields of word puzzles and cryptograms. Cherie put on her thinking cap and redefined what makes a good word search with original themes and some creative spelling. We are proud to report that the books are now available in thousands of book, gift and toy stores, being enjoyed by avid puzzlers across the globe.

We hope you're able to take some time and enjoy our newest edition to the *Armchair Puzzlers* family.

Enjoy!
Bob Moog

4

Introduction

CROSSWORDS

When I was in college I lived in a dorm and I owned one piece of furniture: a big, comfy, overstuffed armchair. When my roommates weren't sitting in it, I used the chair primarily for two things: listening to music and doing crossword puzzles (often at the same time).

It wasn't until much later that I discovered that I come from a long line of devoted, diligent and distinguished (at least in my mind!) solvers on my mother's side, including my great-grandmother, my grandfather, my grandmother and my mother. (My grandmother says that for decades she never actually started a crossword puzzle but finished hundreds, thoughtfully left half done by my grandfather.)

I'm happy to report that my crossword-loving lineage helped me construct many of the puzzles included in this book. My 12-year-old son Joe tried out a few of the puzzles (his first crosswords ever), and my grandmother, Frances Crone, did too. With this book and a writing implement in hand, I encourage you to head for your favorite chair. I hope that you get there before someone else does, and that you enjoy this collection of crosswords from the *Armchair Puzzlers* series.

Jeff Pinsker

WORD PUZZLES & CRYPTOGRAMS

Pql hvicprxven cwuubla jz pqja srrd hrzpejz pql alhvlp pr lplvzeb irwpq. Rdei, pqep'a ez rklvapeplnlzp. Swp pqli evl e nleza pr dllcjzx irwpq jz irwv bjgl. Hwvjrwa?

Hwvjrajpi nleza "pql ywlap grv hrzpjzwrwa blevzjzx." Si hrzapezpbi blevzjzx, tl dllc rwv svejza irwzx ezf ehpjkl. J dzrt nezi clrcbl tqr fr hvicprxven cwuubla ezf

Introduction

pqli'vl ebb ea irwpqgwb ea acvjzx hqjhdlza ezf ea aqevc ea pehda. Pqli'vl ebar ebb vrhdlp ahjlzpjapa ezf Zrslb Cvjul tjzzlva ezf Aqedlaclevlez ehprva. Ezf pqli rtl jp ebb pr hrwzpblaa qrwva aclzp arbkjzx hvicprxven cwuubla.

Jp'a irwv hwvjrajpi pqep tjbb fvjkl irw pr arbkl pql cwuubla jz pqja srrd. J qrcl irw qekl gwz - ezf vlnlnslv pr eccbi pqep hwvjrajpi pr irwv lklvifei bjgl!

Best wishes.
Maria Llull

WORD SEARCHES

There's a lot of fun packed into the word search section of this collection. In fact, there are 35 fun-filled word search puzzles sure to entertain and, most importantly, perplex you. From types of suits in "Suit Yourself" to types of cars in "American Idle," you'll need to use your super-sleuthing skills to find the 840 words buried in this section. Keep an eye out for words that run horizontally, vertically, diagonally, backwards and forwards, but always in a straight line.

So, kick back, relax and have fun! You may even learn a thing or two while you're at it. Who says sitting down means you're a slouch? The next time someone tells you to get out of that chair, ask that person if he/she can list the names of 24 different types of cats.

Now, on your mark, get set . . . SIT!
Cherie Martorana

6

Armchair Puzzlers™

CROSSWORDS

✕ ✕

Sink Back and Solve Away!™

✗ Sit On It ✗

ACROSS
1 "Up and ___ ___"
5 You sit on it
10 You sit on it
14 Opposite of mini
15 One who inflicts cruelty
17 You sit on it
18 Hormone that speeds heartbeats
19 Slow ship (abbr.)
20 "___ ___ Lay Dying" (Faulkner)
21 Builds
22 Flow's partner
24 Catch in the act
27 Sounds of surprise
28 "Stretch" cars
30 Horn
34 Proofreader
36 Two-person hoops game (three words)
40 Settled in
42 Locks up
43 Russian urns
45 Gold standards
46 Olympic treasure
47 "___ ___ who is without sin cast ... "
48 Arthur
51 Egyptian god of music and revelry
53 Staff member's compensation (abbr.)
54 More than needed
57 Rare woman's name
59 Type of music
62 American born of Japanese parents
63 Selfs
64 Peru's bean
65 Spike
66 Fast drink
67 Between "yoos" and "doubleyoos"
68 Listens
69 French battle site
70 Contraction

DOWN
1 Envoys (abbr.)
2 Tight
3 Radicalism
4 31 DOWN'S alma mater (abbr.)
5 Accountants (abbr.)
6 Swedish explorer
7 Dep. (antonym)
8 UK's "ize"
9 Descartes
10 Instruction
11 City of N. Africa or New York
12 Year divider
13 Full- or half-court
16 Vehicle
20 Clear of blame
23 You sit on it
25 US eye doctors' group
26 You sit on them
28 Eye part
29 Concept
31 Nerd
32 Area
33 Gets used to (variant)
35 Book work
37 Small private chapels
38 Holland (abbr.)
39 To be (Latin)
41 Dullness
44 Clever trick
48 You sit on it
49 Banish
50 Where ships belong (two words)
52 You sit on it
55 You sit on it
56 Small islands in England
58 Regarding (two words)
60 Prayer closer
61 History
64 56, in ancient Rome

8

✗ Bit by Bit ✗

ACROSS

1 Pleads
5 Ties up
10 Flower holder
14 As to (two words)
15 Bathsheba's husband
16 Church word
17 Group of players
18 South African language group
19 Solid ground
20 Agile
22 Teases
24 Urban dwelling (abbr.)
26 Snakelike fish (plural)
27 Palm leaf used for writing in India
28 Moines starter
29 Attempt
30 Came to the surface with "up"
34 Fervent religious follower
36 A small fragment
37 Jay of *The Tonight Show*
38 Irregularly indented
39 1/8 of a dollar
40 Oyster product
41 Canyon tops
42 Binary digit
43 Feudal landholder
44 Took care of the kids
46 Actors org.
47 The self
48 Family member (abbr.)
49 Type measure

50 Onto, slang
51 Type of tire
54 Shelter
56 First word of a magical pair
57 Warning
59 Beers
62 Secluded valley
63 Chaucer's word for harm (variant)
64 Not evens
65 Uses needle and thread
66 Pops
67 Concordes (abbr.)

DOWN

1 Short scene
2 Compass direction (abbr.)
3 Famous burial site (two words)
4 Half (prefix)
5 Elastic
6 Aloud
7 Yearns for
8 Consume
9 No-run game
10 Expensive things
11 _____ *Called Horse*, Richard Harris film
12 Mailed
13 Completes

21 European measure (variant)
23 Priest's vestment
24 Action word modifier
25 Illinois city
30 Bridle's mouth piece
31 Rental properties
32 Infuriate
33 A small portion of food
35 Mesopotamians
36 Chewed off
39 Sharp drill part
40 Heathen

42 Narrative songs
43 Leaves the premises
45 Ocean
46 Leone or Madre
49 Address a court
51 Shreds of cloth
52 Adept
53 Made a picture
55 New Mexican art colony
58 Zodiac sign
60 Time zone (abbr.)
61 Draft org.

9

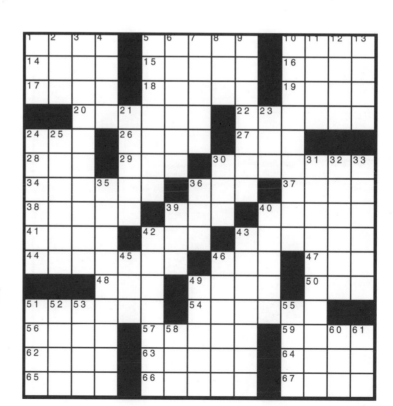

Four Corners

ACROSS

1   Ella's nonsense
5   "Hairy" political party
9   Word with "cotta" or "firma"
11 Clip
12 Walden-ophile
14 Twister
17 Objects with four corners
19 First part of a Four Corners state
20 Squid's product
21 Object with four corners
22 Sulk
23 *A Chorus Line* number
24 Naval ship initials
25 Covers with a certain fabric
26 Skillful
29 Four Corners state
30 Physics lab (abbr.)
31 The boss
32 All (prefix)
34 Uses crayons
37 Japanese poem
38 Lillian, affectionately
39 Umberto of *The Name of the Rose*
41 Ocean (abbr.)
42 Four Corners state with 19 ACROSS
45 Statesman, for short
46 First state (abbr.)
47 Not as wet
48 "You ___ so beautiful..."
49 Four Corners state
52 White water pursuit
55 "___ ___, Jose!"
56 More unusual
57 Leaves
58 Scraps of food

DOWN

1   Shelved, in a store
2   Stock paper work, for short
3   Lengths x widths
4   Calm
5   Who, possessive form
6   Him companion
7   Fleming
8   Cereal, for hippies
10 Octavian's month
11 Suffix with gang or mob
12 Duet plus one
13 Hair treatment
15 Inward dimension
16 Is indebted
18 Vegas, but not Angeles
22 Seussian kangaroo's refrain (two words)
25 Material that produces power
27 Stinky
28 Made from poppies
31 Four Corners state
32 Western movie
33 Standing around
34 Roman statesman and speaker
35 Fixes
36 Contempt
37 Before "little lamb" (two words)
38 52, in Rome
40 Designer Cassini
43 Writers O'Brien and Ferber
44 Internal photo
50 Animals' home
51 Obligated to pay
53 Four-term president (abbr.)
54 Vietnamese holiday

10

✶ Seven Little Men ✶

ACROSS

1 Education place (abbr.)
4 Deli delicacies
10 Radio types
13 Pigeon sound
14 Navel fruit
15 Zip from place to place
16 One (prefix)
17 Titled peers
18 Woman's name
19 Little man
21 Little man
23 French Anthonys
25 Abominable snowmen
26 Chicago airport code
27 Computer instructions
30 Auto journey
33 One power more than square
34 Gwendolyn, to friends
38 Fairy tale starter
39 Permit
40 Thoroughbred Ridge
41 Coral islands
42 Little man
43 Academic credit
44 Cried
45 Odor
46 Firmament
50 Diving duck
53 Milky-skinned creature

54 Depending (on)
58 Splashless sound
59 Most frozen
62 Hawaiian garland
63 One of XII popes
64 Medic
65 Sun, in Madrid
66 Until now
67 Little man
68 Tiny worker

DOWN

1 Underwater breathing apparatus
2 The Barbarian
3 Lift
4 Celebratory conflagration
5 On all sides
6 Anne's green roof part
7 Sign up (abbr.)
8 Big size (abbr.)
9 Official meeting (abbr.)
10 Group of ships
11 Actress Gaynor
12 Remains
15 Run away
20 Horses' feet
22 The Science Guy
24 Molds
28 Reed instrument

29 Misty
30 Little man
31 Genetic info carrier (abbr.)
32 Frozen
33 Hoof on pavement sound
34 Little man
35 Fruit of the vine
36 Morally bad
37 Of the country (abbr.)
39 Masses of lymphoid tissue behind the nose
44 Harmless cyst

45 Steamy
46 Little man
47 *Phantom Menace* princess
48 Regarding
49 Special ones (abbr.)
51 Greek island
52 Fable maker
55 Ingrid's *Casablanca* character
56 Sign gas
57 Covered with gold
60 Army officer (abbr.)
61 Solid water

11

✶ Nyms ✶

ACROSS

1 A British boy (two words)
5 Crustacean
9 Florida town
14 African nation
15 Loony
16 Gourmet mushroom
17 Region
18 Gumbo vegetable
19 Straighten
20 Nothing
22 Religion of strict adherence
24 Houston ballplayer
25 Make beloved
26 Data studier
28 Aleutian island
32 Nym with same sound
34 Broadcast sound signals
36 Clothing protector
37 Hwys.
38 Opposite nym
39 Makes corrections
41 Tight
42 Keyboard button (abbr.)
43 Antlered animal
44 False names
47 Assisted
49 Pay increase
53 Fake name nym
57 More confident
58 San Antonio fort
59 Neckwear (plural)
61 Suddenly bright star
62 Of the Muses
63 Singular
64 What you catch a butterfly with (two words)
65 Woman's clothing item
66 NCOs
67 Similar nym, with "nym"

DOWN

1 Appliance manufacturer
2 Zhivago's love and others
3 Resident of 28 ACROSS
4 Explanatory image
5 Clump
6 South Korea (abbr.)
7 Initial nym
8 Planks
9 D-Day beach
10 Mountainous state
11 Lacking moisture
12 Late night host
13 Trebek
21 Awards
23 Lockjaw
25 Tarzan portrayer Ron and family
27 Plus
29 Prong
30 Playthings
31 Military branch (abbr.)
32 Pelt
33 Off-Broadway award
35 Speaks
36 Sleeping furniture
38 Car org.
40 Emotional shocks
41 Cleaning
44 Fuss
45 Slow tempos, in music
46 Dry heat baths
48 Worshipped objects
50 Sardonic literary style
51 Single digit number
52 Muse of poetry
53 One of NASA's Payload Assist Modules (abbr.)
54 Insult
55 Without difficulty
56 Liquefy
60 Instant messaging sign-off (abbr.)

12

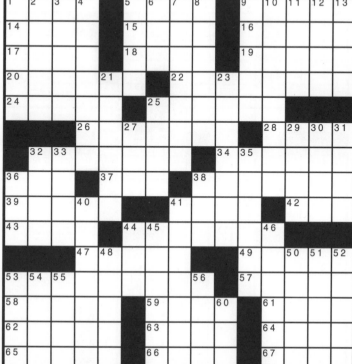

Olfactory Sensations

ACROSS

1 Olfactory sensation
5 Arrive
9 Pawn off
14 Rub to clean
15 Grand Nashville site
16 Positive olfactory sensation
17 Reindeer herder
18 Gripper
19 Anagram and synonym of notes
20 Mary-Kate or Ashley
22 Childhood innoculation (abbr.)
24 Kind
25 Written out
28 Responds
30 Idaho product, informally
31 Demonstrations (two words)
33 Accustomed to
35 Successful Broadway sign (abbr.)
36 Soldiers (abbr.)
40 Absence of (prefix)
41 Act of wiping away to correct
44 Male sheep
45 Maintain
47 Resembling (suffix)
48 Loco
50 Negative olfactory sensation
53 Heavenly inhabitant
54 Avers
57 Tactile
59 Corn comes on it

60 Simultaneous computer game (abbr.)
62 Asian palm tree
63 Wear away
65 Biblical high priest
67 Possess information
70 Grandmas
71 Intrusive
72 So. Cal. school (abbr.)
73 Eighth Greek letter
74 Fourth letters
75 Equal

DOWN

1 Wise bird
2 Across (prefix)
3 Convenient
4 One who responds
5 Desire
6 Gives an opinion
7 Married woman's title
8 Looked at
9 Plump up
10 Spanish gold
11 Type of Greek architecture
12 Had an olfactory sensation (variant)
13 Duties
21 Carefree activity
23 Before the fact, with "a"
25 Negative olfactory sensation
26 Tipsy boat
27 Analyze by cutting open

29 Small African snake
32 US's biggest toy chain (abbr.)
34 Least wet
37 Positive olfactory sensation
38 Ancient Cretan city
39 Olfactory sensation
42 Michigan city with "Arbor"
43 Maternal relative
46 Time zone in CA (abbr.)
49 Advanced without being noticed (two words)
51 Nobel-winning nun

52 Coffin carrier
54 Positive olfactory sensation
55 First five biblical books
56 What "This Old Man's" dog gets (two words)
58 Radiation photography
61 Mail
64 Recording medium (abbr.)
66 Woman's name
68 15 ACROSS modifier
69 Armed conflict

13

✶ Hi-tech Talk ✶

ACROSS

1 Taxi
4 Beantown
10 Hi-tech box (abbr.)
13 Of the fields (abbr.)
14 Charge
15 Punch
16 Fish eggs
17 Group of teams
18 An example of 17 ACROSS (abbr.)
19 Small bird
21 Delicately charming
23 Mature married women
24 Tyler
25 Old hi-tech operating system
26 At any time
31 English region
34 Oceanic boundary
35 Irish rebel group (abbr.)
36 Closes
37 Hi-tech data medium
38 Makes narrow
41 Follows orders
43 Hi-tech typing unit
44 Word with "status"
45 Middle school subject (abbr.)
46 Vending machine for food
50 Full-length garment
53 Hi-tech portables
54 Add to the work force
55 Slow movement (music)
58 Penn. school (abbr.)
59 Fusses
60 Disney remembered them
61 Narrow water channel (abbr.)
62 Hi-tech memory (abbr.)
63 Jim Crow-era victim Till
64 Curve shape

DOWN

1 Bounce off of
2 Ancient Greek marketplace
3 Hall of Famer George
4 Inflatable toy
5 Seas
6 Leafs through
7 Small, powerful boat
8 Ohio school (abbr.)
9 Unnecessary
10 Family group
11 Green action
12 Hideous
15 Whine
20 Church calendar
22 This form of isn't isn't proper
26 Cut
27 Toppers
28 See (Latin)
29 Jealousy
30 Cincinnati's team
31 Hi-tech data storage medium
32 Art Deco artist
33 Differ
34 "Dear" singer
36 Remain the same
39 Eases
40 Kansas town
41 Remote settlement
42 A type of camp
44 Cute
46 Seaweed (Latin)
47 Hi-tech hand-held device
48 Scheduled mtgs.
49 Russian rulers
50 Burn on the outside
51 Verdi opera
52 Originating in
56 Not bright
57 Air (abbr.)

14

✕ Rhymes of All Sizes ✕

ACROSS

1 Cheery
5 English-speaking North American
10 Hefty animal rhyme, with 58 DOWN
13 Big shot's car, for short
14 Big transport rhyme, with 47 ACROSS
15 Military vehicle
16 Smelting residue
17 System of beliefs
18 Jason's ship
19 Pakistani city
21 Loafers
23 Buddy
25 Direct sales organization
26 Muscle paralysis and tremors
27 Military locale (abbr.)
28 Alcindor
29 Pay for
30 Moves on all fours
32 Belonging to him
33 Killer whale
37 Eur. measures, for short
38 Seuss's wears socks
39 Athenian politician or NY baseballer
40 Post-D-Day battle site
41 Youngster
42 Hardened tissue
43 Cartoon deputy
45 Old French coin
46 "___ we there yet?"
47 See 14 ACROSS

49 Belonging to males
50 Sum (abbr.)
51 Instruction book
52 Nicaraguan leader
54 Branch of the armed forces (abbr.)
55 Gas flow regulator
57 First 4 of 26
60 Simple, unsuspecting person (variant)
61 Consumed
62 Kill
63 Sick
64 Small playing surface rhyme, with 35 DOWN
65 Townshend or Sampras

DOWN

1 Literary monogram
2 Petroleum product
3 Tiny sphere rhyme
4 Hindu exercise system
5 Small room extensions
6 Thin
7 Envious color
8 Abbr. for 14 ACROSS
9 Subject for Sophocles
10 Tariffs
11 Mad
12 Boxing endings

15 High toy rhyme
20 Passageways
22 Dapper person
23 Back wear (plural)
24 Arabic demon (variant)
29 Repair
31 Coca-Cola builder Robert
32 Burning
34 Capable of being told
35 See 64 ACROSS
36 Photographer Adams
38 Low clouds
39 Effect producer

41 Dozens
42 Satisfied
44 Turkish leader
45 Waitperson
47 Of primary importance
48 Traditional kingdom loser (two words)
49 Very, in music
51 Local bond, for short
53 Catch one's breath, from shock
56 Sigh of relief
58 See 10 ACROSS
59 Coloring substance

15

Something Fishy

ACROSS

1 U2's lead singer
5 Half of a NY prison
9 Sitting fish?
14 College (abbr.)
15 Islamic chieftain
16 Self-evident principle
17 Shoe-bottom fish?
18 Mexican food
19 Detroit's team
20 There are four in Monopoly (abbr.)
22 Praise
24 Fish with a blade?
27 Spanish name
28 Story
32 Nasal cavity
33 Baldwin
34 Get caught on
35 Noisy sleepers
37 Steal
39 The square root of four
40 A large degree
41 Leppard
43 This makes 41 ACROSS's music loud (abbr.)
46 Cry
48 House lister
52 Instrumental fish?
54 Surveys
56 Web-footed bird
57 Python alumnus Idle
58 Stain
59 Enticed
60 Command
62 Writing implement
63 Type of acid
66 Mayberry character
68 1/16 ounce
72 Blue jean material
73 World's longest river
74 Supreme Court Justice Warren
75 Move to music
76 Shout
77 Measures of rotational speed (abbr.)

DOWN

1 Group conveyance
2 Yoko
3 Soccer score
4 Reverse
5 Tennis units
6 Words with "Yankee Doodle Dandy"
7 Silver metal
8 Organizer fish?
9 Stanford city, with "Alto"
10 Lives
11 South American river
12 Against
13 Start of a British vessel name (abbr.)
21 Changes the reading
23 Unscramble
24 Draft org. (abbr.)
25 Family
26 Black cuckoo
27 Mas' partners
29 Hill member
30 Legal code
31 Conceit
36 Equilateral parallelograms
38 Snoopy is one
42 Blundering fish?
43 Lincoln, to friends
44 Ruin
45 Greek letter
47 Porch
48 Q-U connectors
49 Craggy hill
50 Sugary suffix
51 Angry color
53 Having pleasant natural features
55 Chicken dish (two words)
61 Hemispheric roof
62 Rind
63 Find a sum
64 Word with "culpa"
65 Place to stay
67 Sick
69 Type of music
70 Limb
71 Soccer league (abbr.)

16

ACROSS

1 Big 5, without "u"
5 Bowling score
8 Long and dusty (plural)
13 Paid for
16 Underdog's victory
17 Football score
18 Indian leader
19 Come out of
20 CIA's cousin
21 Split apart
22 Curve
24 Pitcher's stat (abbr.)
26 Accountant (abbr.)
29 Bowling score
33 Oklahoma or Ohio college (abbr.)
36 Rock's partner
38 Theodore and Franklin
40 TV Kate's partner
42 Q-U connectors
43 Bowling score
44 Football scores
47 Distant
48 Plaything
49 Egyptian leader
50 Procedure (abbr.)
51 Accounting system (abbr.)
53 Not safe
56 Soccer or hockey score
58 Beer's cousin
61 Hold on, with "fast" (two words)

65 Beaux _____
67 Strict disciplinarians
69 This puzzle's theme
70 Tennis score
71 Every
72 "The Luck of Roaring Camp" author
73 Before a spike (plural)
74 Kanga's pouch inhabitant

DOWN

1 Sparkling Italian city
2 Poems with an epic theme
3 Chits
4 As directed (two words)
5 Seed covering
6 Shirt presser
7 The latest events
8 Baseball score
9 *Aida*, e.g.
10 Tennis great
11 Bruce or Laura
12 Wall board
14 ___ *Come Undone*
15 Genetic carrier
23 Soviet Republic (abbr.)
24 Achieve with difficulty
25 New software versions (abbr.)
26 Vessel

27 Salk's vaccine wiped it out
28 U of F player on a side street(?)
30 Matadors' opponents
31 Parks, et al.
32 Agave plant
33 Lemony counts
34 Wander
35 Employers
37 Abner or Kim
39 Government's green group
41 Ferber or St. Vincent Millay
45 Clothing retailer

46 Sold out sign
52 At the ready
54 Standard quantities
55 Weighty measure
56 Cut
57 Killer whale
58 Unit of electric current
59 Kampuchean neighbor
60 Weird-sounding Great Lake
62 Rip
63 French town
64 Norwegian capital
66 Look
68 Explosive (abbr.)

17

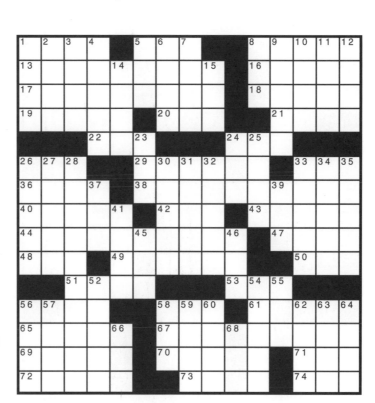

✶ Playthings ✶

ACROSS

1 Toy with rules
5 Summer drinks
9 Beats
14 Prayer ending
15 Spherical toy
16 ____ nous
17 Young female
18 Church part
19 Baking need
20 Capture
22 Brit. mil. award (abbr.)
24 Movie player
25 Making indistinct
28 I found it!
30 Big
31 Painting holders, in process
33 Familiarize
35 Sibling, for short
36 *Gone With The Wind* estate
40 Eggs
41 Quick swim
43 Score (plural abbr.)
45 Unruly group
46 Place to buy this puzzle's theme items
48 Ordinary (abbr.)
50 Take the place of
52 Beetle
55 Thorny plants
56 Ridiculous
59 Sky color (noun)
61 What this puzzle is about
62 Poetic contraction
64 Oil cartel
65 Myanmar
67 And so ons (abbr.)
69 Little *Sesame Street* monster
73 Grads (abbr.)
74 Riding toy
75 Humanoid toy
76 Native American structure
77 Aide (abbr.)
78 Oklahoma town

DOWN

1 Prank
2 Friend, in France
3 Volatile
4 Make bigger
5 Counting devices
6 *Scooby-Doo* character
7 Heights (pl. abbr.)
8 Toy with runners
9 Contaminate
10 Join (abbr.)
11 Kitchen top
12 Wheeled toy
13 Spanish missionary
21 Tendency
23 Takes care of (two words)
25 Ulysses' protagonist
26 Insect before metamorphosis
27 Auto need
29 Q-U connectors
32 Take a small drink
34 Diatribe
37 What a good toy does
38 Lassos
39 Bottomless chasm
42 For each
44 Loose rocks at a slope's bottom
47 Baton Rouge sch. (abbr.)
49 Talk (and talk)
51 Give in
53 Fold
54 Building toys
56 At the plate (two words)
57 Pear-shaped synthetic gem
58 Maple tree product
60 Make mad
63 McEntire
66 French Mrs.
68 "My country" follower
70 Code for London's airport
71 1051, to Nero
72 Aged

18

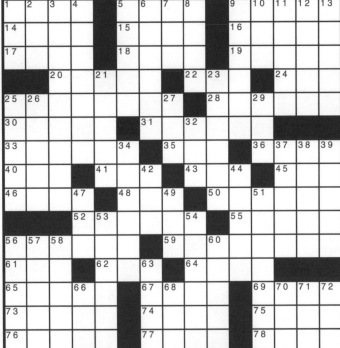

✗ Who Let 'Em Out? ✗

ACROSS

1 Short poem
5 Primates
9 Mongoose's foe
14 "___ _ penny, pick it up ... "
15 Pineapple company
16 Acrylic fiber
17 Powder
18 Toss up in the air
19 Cheek makeup
20 Mentally clear
22 Crone
24 Playful activity
25 Capable of being forgiven
28 Irritated
30 Martin's sidekick
31 Hemingway
33 Lassie's breed
35 Relating to (suffix)
36 USSR, to Boris
40 Women's movement legislation (abbr.)
41 Terrier breed (nickname)
44 Garden tool
45 Touches lightly with paint
47 Bruin great Bobby
48 Browns
50 Dozing
53 Scorched (variant)
54 Snoopy's breed
57 Marcus
59 Popeye's "goil's" second name
60 Bat wood
62 Knitting stitches
63 Repetitious training
65 Devout
67 Indian Ocean vessel
70 Sound on Old MacDonald's farm
71 Valley flower
72 Goddess of wine
73 Jean material
74 Hardy's girl of the D'Urbervilles
75 Smile

DOWN

1 Real or violin ending
2 Government agency for narcotics (abbr.)
3 Retriever breed
4 Of a gap of empty space (variant)
5 Wing it
6 French breed
7 Small, impish creature
8 Adam's third son
9 Welsh breeds
10 Spanish gold
11 Fake out
12 Scoundrel
13 Finish off, with "bring to" (two words)
21 This puzzle's theme's genus
23 Earhart
25 Curved
26 Australian town or Star Wars senator
27 New country near Ethiopia
29 Govt. agency for commerce (abbr.)
32 King Cole
34 French schools
37 One who holds something dear
38 Horn-like structure
39 Irritants
42 Mineral lode
43 Glowing fire part
46 Droop
49 English breed
51 Downhill race
52 Students
54 Was an omen for
55 High nest (variant)
56 UFO driver
58 Giuliani and others
61 Stop
64 52, in ancient Rome
66 Compete
68 USN's secret service (abbr.)
69 Was victorious

19

✗ Subjects ✗

ACROSS

1 Fishing need
5 Actor's place
10 Subject
14 Source of annoyance
15 Giant
16 Mixture
17 Detective's project
18 Disconnect, aboard ship
19 Alaskan city
20 Nervous (two words)
22 Currency of Sierra Leone
24 P.E.
26 Heap
27 Between (prefix)
28 Chaney
29 Shoe measurement
30 Norwegian city
31 Gets up
33 Where a subj. is taught
34 Cashews and pecans
38 Gathers
39 Delivery service (abbr.)
40 Glycerin starter
41 To be (Latin)
42 Air above Earth
43 Subject, with 5 DOWN
44 Head scourge
46 Bath
47 Number of cards in a deck (Roman numeral)
48 Famous Lama
50 Top-notch (two words)
51 Self-governing (abbr.)
52 Salty
53 Voting need
55 College subject (abbr.)
56 Scandinavian
58 Assistant
61 Drink in one gulp
62 Talks informally
63 Estate recipient
64 A small amount
65 TV awards
66 Annapolis institution (abbr.)

DOWN

1 English broadcaster (abbr.)
2 Car assn.
3 Sleeping disorders
4 "___ Angel"
5 See 43 ACROSS
6 Prickly sensation
7 The subject of Kilmer's famous poem (two words)
8 Thai word for chicken
9 Subject
10 In an unvarying tone
11 By oneself
12 Stopwatch, e.g.
13 Garden tools
21 Fencing swords
23 Not commissioned (abbr.)
24 Blinding brightness
25 Times long past
30 Military training school (abbr.)
32 Subject
33 Secret agent
35 Gas and electric, e.g.
36 Rail rider
37 State of matter
39 Small guitar, for short
40 Prestigious prize
42 Subject
43 Lacking natural light
45 Bond creator, to friends
46 Pleasantly warm
48 Russian country house
49 Audible
50 Variation of Abraham
52 Separate religious group
54 Hawaiian island
57 Unit of electrical resistance
59 Noise
60 Time period

The "Spices" of Life

ACROSS

1 Tennis great
5 Couch potato
9 Storybook elephant
14 Thin strip of land
15 Monster
16 Make amends
17 Oceanic spice
18 Pull up unwanted plants
19 Biblical verb
20 Commands
22 Desert
24 Actor Gibson
25 Stop
26 Cheap piece of jewelry
28 Outpatient facility
30 Small unit of matter
34 2001 computer
37 Michigan county
38 Play type
39 Texas city (two words)
41 17 ACROSS companion
42 Host Philbin
43 Spice measurer
46 Hard-working insect
47 Stand
48 Easels
49 Globe
51 Wipe away
56 Govt. food org.
59 Yeses
60 Builds

61 Purple color or flower
63 Plot
65 Railroad boards
66 Alas' partner
67 Bawdy
68 Concept
69 Layers of wood
70 Needle holes
71 Glimpse

DOWN

1 Org.
2 Almost as good as a strike
3 German woman's name
4 Suffix with "kitchen"(plural)
5 Arrows' partners
6 Shirt size (abbr.)
7 Pizza spice
8 Arabian nomad
9 Pesto spice
10 Money machine
11 Sonic sound
12 Place a bet
13 Movie holder
21 School break
23 British channel
26 Removable drill piece
27 Wyatt
29 Mekong Buddhist
31 Spanish snack
32 Portent

33 Shopping place
34 Spice relative
35 Toward the side away from the wind
36 Women's tour
38 Thicker
40 Broadcasts
41 Pea holder
43 Church spire
44 Green spice companion
45 First number
48 Bashful

50 Places in a container
52 Lace again
53 Substances with a pH less than seven
54 Soak in liquid
55 Writing assignment
56 Wing motion
57 Pickling spice
58 Sport, with "jai"
60 Finishes
62 Aviation hero
64 Overwhelming admiration

21

✗ Classical Puns ✗

ACROSS

1 Old hoops league (abbr.)
4 Sick
7 Principled
14 Infectious disease
16 Classical shopping need, with 5 DOWN
17 Female performer
18 Army bigwig
19 See 34 ACROSS
20 Half of Ms. Gabor's name
22 Snuggle
23 Usefulness
25 Roman garb (plural)

29 Tree
30 Manager
34 Classical clip joint, with 19 ACROSS
36 Word with "dog"
39 Baltimore bird
40 Classical bike grips, with 52 DOWN
41 Required
42 New Testament group (abbr.)
43 First lady
44 Rims
45 Sound of discovery
47 Human-eating giants

49 Playing field
52 See 2 DOWN
56 Classical children's game, with 60 DOWN
57 Short sleeps
61 '60s movement
63 Break open
65 Musical flourish
66 Mineral source
67 Wade's opponent
68 More cunning
69 Tennis divider
70 Question

DOWN

1 Latin school word
2 Classical brew, with 52 ACROSS
3 Choir voice
4 Wrath
5 See 16 ACROSS
6 TV pooch
7 One of a dozen
8 Senator Lott
9 Bee product
10 Freezes
11 Ownership document (abbr.)
12 Asian inland sea
13 Lovett

15 Alsatian artist
21 Every
23 Futile
24 Mischievous child
25 Steak type
26 Rowed
27 Norwegian composer
28 Home
30 Storage container
31 Command
32 Sifter
33 Monica of tennis fame
35 Primary color
37 17th Greek letter
38 Moses' brother
42 Kettle for boiling (variant)
45 Game's choice besides "a truth" (two words)
46 Yo!
48 Polite man, for short
50 Two words before "a hammer"
51 Get used to
52 See 40 ACROSS
53 Organic compound
54 Small ornamental case
55 Upset
58 Distinctive atmosphere
59 Paid experts (abbr.)
60 See 56 ACROSS
62 What 61 ACROSS is against
64 Domestic animal

22

✗ 7 Cs ✗

ACROSS
1 Pillar (abbr.)
4 "__ __ Papa!" (gambling slang)
10 Unruly group
13 Resort
14 Planet
15 Mister, in München
16 Reject, in apparel (abbr.)
17 Grows past the expected hour
18 Proud father's first two words
19 Warnings
21 Eskimo homes
23 Capital of Sudan
25 Type of criminals
26 With "-d" or "-vous"
27 Leaves out
29 Climber
32 Joints
33 Look at
36 Roof part
37 Rises
38 C1, mad
39 Mimic
40 Wedge-shaped proofing mark
41 Scorches
42 Type of newspaper
43 Tennis unit
44 Movie need
47 C2, blind person's helper?
52 Sickness

53 To stand for
54 Pig noise
55 Silver State
58 Adenosine triphosphate (abbr.)
59 Samovars
60 Chest part
61 Unable to communicate in English (abbr.)
62 Plaything
63 C3, awake from being knocked out
64 An indeterminate amount

DOWN
1 C4, sensitive to waves
2 Talk show queen
3 Newly hatched insect
4 C5, goodbye
5 Speaker
6 Chinese island
7 Compass direction
8 Large cask for wine
9 Changes into bone
10 And I (two words)
11 Welles
12 Orchestra section

15 Small mountains
20 Bert's buddy
22 Obtains
24 C6, with "monkey do"
28 Swimming competition
29 One of seven
30 Spigot
31 St.
32 Marx
33 Make a mistake
34 Japanese currency
35 Norton and Mister
37 C7, decide later
38 Take over a dance partner (two words)

40 Super accessory
41 They're not choosers
42 Circular objects
43 Nastier
44 Schnoz
45 Egypt's capital
46 One way to order eggs
48 Tweety's words, without an impediment
49 Lady or Ross
50 Frequently
51 Nomad
56 Interjections
57 Tub

23

✶ Picture This ✶

ACROSS

1 Camera output, for short (plural)
5 Eastern European
9 Bike pusher
14 Woman of Green Gables
15 Taboo (two words)
16 Selassie
17 Wings
18 Not home
19 Killer whales
20 Sweet red sauce
22 Rude
24 Leaning Tower-er
25 Rotten (two words)
26 Magi (two words)
28 Finished
32 Trim
35 One-horse carriage
36 Picture taker
38 Smooth over, as with difficulties (two words)
40 In the ____ (on the spot) (two words)
41 Hidden
42 Especially
43 Compass direction
44 Cat sound
45 One who teases
48 Witches' threats
50 Cheesy chip
54 Shoed card game
57 Holy
58 German sub
59 Drains
61 Angelic circle
62 Night shot need
63 Rope snarl
64 At any time
65 Soft fabrics
66 Cleopatra biters
67 Camera part

DOWN

1 African American org.
2 Chou
3 Small insects
4 Teeter-totter
5 Take a quick pic
6 Small elevation
7 Body science
8 Sea journey
9 Picture
10 Noble domains
11 Dotted cubes
12 Woe is me
13 Fewer
21 As one
23 Mix
25 Tidy
27 It makes a camera click
29 Duck formations
30 Time periods
31 Rank
32 Camera need
33 Dies ____ (Latin)
34 Kansas canine
37 Greek goddess of wisdom
39 TV staple
40 Asian nomads of the 4th century
42 Ottoman rulers
46 Icy state
47 Author's daughter
49 Ways
51 Desire
52 Woman of Troy
53 Smells
54 Polish
55 Having skill
56 Fuel
57 Concordes
60 Flashbulb sound

24

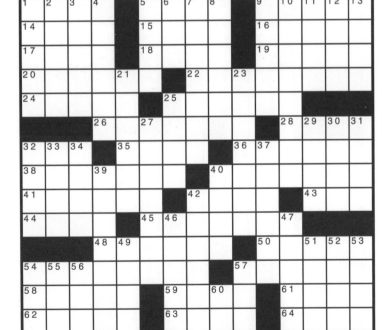

✶ Lazy English ✶

ACROSS

1 Actor Alan
5 Lazy PM
9 Grouch
14 German car
15 Hot and dry
16 Safe
17 State
18 Restaurant list
19 Plenty
20 Compass direction
22 Head skin
24 Lazy need
27 Gather ·
28 Lazy little weight
32 Decorate
33 Mellower sax
34 Reverberate
35 Entrance
37 Chicago trains
39 Lazy sweetheart
40 Golf score
41 Fall behind
43 Point at
46 Lazy sibling
48 Amiable
52 Lazy holiday
54 Stair
56 Make parallel
57 Gunslinger Wyatt
58 Friends
59 Looked at
60 Contraction
62 Lazy moment
63 Put a top on

66 Nick's explorer
68 Lazy preposition
72 Take a gun away
73 The clink
74 "_ ___ a man
with seven wives"
75 Sectors
76 Jedi knight
77 Handle

DOWN

1 Travelers' group
2 Lazy affection
3 Ike (abbr.)
4 Runway
5 Moniker
6 Wrath
7 Tree adornment
8 Teach
9 Indy shape
10 Representative
piece
11 Drinking vessel
12 Every
13 Hwy.
21 _____ elves
23 Zeus's son
24 Prattle on
25 Lyric poem
26 Pull
27 Cheer
29 JFK's first word
in Berlin
30 Lazy however
31 Two or more
eras

36 British chips
38 Uncivilized
42 Relating to the
Milky Way
43 Chopping tool
44 "__ _ Yankee
Doodle Dandy"
45 Spoil
47 Substitute
48 Before CDs
49 Lazy corporation
50 Bigger than
medium (abbr.)
51 Finish

53 Globe
55 The bull (two words)
61 Limbs
62 Long narrative
63 Lazy reason
64 Yoko
65 Ludwig Beethoven
connector
67 Eliminate
69 Med. org.
70 Congressperson
(abbr.)
71 Native American
of Utah

Opposites Attract

ACROSS

1 If this fits, wear it
5 Sugary and opposite (with 5 DOWN)
10 Blue ox or pink pig
14 Freezing and opposite (with 2 DOWN)
15 Tanker
16 Amiss
17 The start of Dickens's "a far, far better thing" (two words)
18 Exorbitant interest
19 Bear's den
20 Prepared, with "up"
22 Late game kick, in football
24 Horse's home
26 Teach
28 Dep. (antonym)
29 Obese and opposite (with 31 DOWN)
32 WWII theater (abbr.)
33 Spinal pains
36 Height impaired and opposite (with 40 DOWN)
41 Yearn for
42 Hayseeds
44 Solo
45 Storm center
46 Hawaiian fish
47 Excite
49 One who plays for dough
51 Entice
53 Colloid
54 DaVinci's "Mona"
56 Squad or talk
57 Opposite of base
59 Angels
61 Type of car
63 Chef
64 Vows
66 Disfigure
69 Final sitting Stuart
70 Sailboat
71 Fitzgerald
72 Famous loch
73 Make void
74 Norwegian city

DOWN

1 Sch. subj.
2 See 14 ACROSS
3 Minority government
4 Old Ford model
5 See 5 ACROSS
6 Sage
7 Evade
8 Poetic contraction
9 Attempt to make the team (two words)
10 Toy airplane wood
11 Look forward to
12 Groom's partner
13 Jane
21 Romeo predecessor
23 Chief Petty Officers, e.g.
24 West Indies island
25 Draw over
27 Office need
30 Gesundheit predecessor
31 See 29 ACROSS
34 Mementoes
35 Pierre's school
37 Twin "hardy" follower
38 Authentic works of art
39 Stirred to anger
40 See 36 ACROSS
43 Trunk type (abbr.)
48 Opposite of tail
50 Type of music
52 Result
54 Sierra follower
55 Presses
56 Sacred song
58 Special appearance
59 Review quickly
60 Water conveyer
62 Catch sight of
65 Opposite of bottom
67 Opposite of well
68 *Little Red Book* author

Barnyard Sounds

ACROSS

1 Major ending
5 Despised
10 Feline sound
14 Canine sound
15 Earthy pigment
16 Solo song
17 Nobleman
18 The Hunter
19 South African currency
20 Golf tournament
22 Takes pleasure in
23 Fume
25 Widens
27 European eagle (variant)
28 Canine sound
29 Deep-sea fish
30 Motor hotels
32 Caregivers
33 Fairy tale starter
37 Beats me, with "know"
38 Bandleader Brown
39 Fishing line
40 Landed servant
41 A small amount
42 Screw-up
43 Uncovered
45 10 ACROSS noisemaker
46 Heart machine output (abbr.)
47 Opens
50 Korsakov companion
52 Duck sound
53 Mexicans
55 Cajole
56 Midwesterner
57 Caps
60 Food thickener
61 Greek island
62 God of love
63 Urges
64 Bovine gland
65 French city

DOWN

1 22 DOWN noisemaker
2 Fit _ _ tee
3 Cruel teaser
4 Musical note
5 Owls
6 Land measure
7 Ordinal number
8 24 DOWN processes
9 Cub Scout group
10 Long races
11 Rub away
12 Porcine noises
13 Lumps
21 Ten Commandments verb
22 Ovine noise
23 Large trucks
24 Wear away
26 Pre-CD music media
31 Rough hockey players
32 Primary color
34 Required
35 Fowl noise
36 Poem of mourning
38 Property owner
39 Protest demonstration
41 British staple
42 Seaman
44 Beijing's airport code
47 Rush forward
48 Non-believer
49 Cut
51 Motor hotel
52 Pier
54 London museum
56 Hospital wing (abbr.)
58 Bovine noise
59 ID number (abbr.)

27

✦ Rhyming Words ✦

ACROSS

1 Baby bed
5 Clock-like rhyme
9 Herbal rhyme
14 Bowling place
15 Deception
16 Oarsman
17 Concept
18 Word of pain
19 Famous grouch
20 Reflective surface
22 Environments
24 Gnaws
25 Hairy
26 Gorges
28 Tart rhyme

32 Eight's homonym
35 Hereditary unit
36 Fought
38 Twins or cats
40 Depending (on)
41 Not moving (two words)
42 Shopping site
43 Cash's boy's name
44 Early video game
45 Winter roof hangers
48 Fleet
50 To stuff with food
54 Those who act incorrectly

57 Genus plural
58 Jargon
59 10¢ worth of rhyme
61 Muhammad, et al.
62 Smart organization
63 Site of Bonaparte's first exile
64 Not wild
65 German city
66 Hind part
67 Skater's jump

DOWN

1 Upward-moving rhyme
2 Half diameters
3 Unable to move
4 To whom checks are sometimes paid
5 Norse god of thunder
6 Chit
7 Mechanical contraption
8 Breathe out
9 Three, to Pierre
10 Inn
11 Ladies' group

12 What carnivores eat
13 Flubs
21 Some Native Americans
23 Samuel Johnson's biographer
25 Coniferous tree
27 Remnant
29 Eye part
30 Food list
31 U2's guitarist
32 Right away (abbr.)
33 Yugoslavian leader
34 Gain from effort
37 Assert
39 Large portion of a drug
40 Risqué
42 Projectile
46 One who piles up wood
47 Musical composition
49 French novel
51 Loosen up
52 Dirty rhyme
53 Painter's need
54 Silent rhyme
55 Day of March madness
56 Misdeeds
57 Stuff
60 Bus. degree (abbr.)

28

✗ Space Race ✗

ACROSS

1 Card suit
5 "Fall _ _ " (REM song)
9 Card suit
14 Russian space name
15 Skin
16 Made a mistake
17 Curves
18 Wrongful act
19 Dahl
20 Mementoes
22 US space name
24 Woman's name
25 Gold
26 Mature name
28 Sleeveless Arabic garments
32 Black and gray bird
35 TV award
36 Element
38 US space name
40 Say again
41 Small pieces of land surrounded by water
42 Impassive
44 Russian space name
45 Couch
46 Tracy
48 Wheat and white
50 King of the Israelites
54 Big Blue
57 Intransitive (abbr.)
58 US space name
59 Hangs out
61 Designate
63 A followers
64 Russian space name
65 Graphic symbol
66 French milk
67 Scrub a space shot
68 Held onto
69 Time periods

DOWN

1 Barton
2 Enticed
3 Mother's brother
4 Spice
5 Chooses
6 New (prefix)
7 US space name
8 The bull (Spanish)
9 Medicine
10 High school dance
11 Middle East resident
12 Sandwich shop, for short
13 Icelandic poetry collection
21 11 DOWN's animals
23 Crazy person
25 Cash dispenser
27 Latin school word
28 Spring month (abbr.)
29 Laser emission
30 Play starter (two words)
31 Gang- or mob- suffix
32 Raised platform
33 Tibetan watchdog, with "lhasa"
34 Dog's cousin
37 Break off
39 Tree part
40 Charged particles
42 Russian space name
43 Patio
46 Offspring
47 Talk on and on and on
49 Hungarian composer and pianist
51 Priest
52 Asian country
53 Eats carefully
54 Rick's true love
55 Goofball
56 12 DOWN spread, for short
58 Polite man, for short
60 Some mammals' hair
62 Floor cleaner

29

✕ Give Me a Sign ✕

ACROSS

1 Words of understanding
5 Right away
9 Horrible
14 Compatriot
15 Wait patiently
16 Complaint
17 Stock mkt. (abbr.)
18 Caused to reproduce
19 Uncontrollable
20 Plaything
22 When most 20 ACROSSES are purchased (abbr.)
24 Dromedary
27 State that starts and ends with the same letter
29 Warning sign
33 Lubricated
34 Ladder step
35 Ireland
36 Banal
37 Toy weapon
39 Girl who enters society formally, informally
40 Pres. after FDR
42 Place for cars
44 Ship name starter
47 Oceanic changes
51 Of the country
55 Red sign
57 Disorderly condition
58 Yellow sign
59 Island nation
60 Diner sign
61 Valuable item
62 Bookworm
64 Legal degree
65 Avarice
68 Singer James
71 Above
75 Sign of submission
76 *Cheers* regular
77 Ivy League school
78 Covered with a certain plant
79 Leak
80 Pop

DOWN

1 Anderson, of Jethro Tull
2 Clever
3 Chicago's metros, informally
4 Upper canines
5 "Dear" follower
6 Term of respect
7 Summer drink
8 Human sign (two words)
9 Taj Mahal site
10 Tropical fish
11 White lie
12 News org. (abbr.)
13 Zeppelin
21 Most elderly
23 Ski bump
24 Camp bed
25 Breathable gas
26 1051, to Caesar
27 Sphere
28 Focal point
30 Cover
31 Miner's find
32 Internet synonym
38 Regular
41 Stopwatch
43 Days of the week
44 So. Cal. school (abbr.)
45 Little, for short
46 Cry
48 Dangerous sounding sign (two words)
49 Time zone (abbr.)
50 Draft org. (abbr.)
52 Road sign x-ings (abbr.)
53 Duration of life
54 Tennis re-do
56 Groups of experts
63 Small whirlpool
64 Illuminator
65 Workout place
66 Brazil's former capital, for short
67 Type of engr. (plural)
69 Rocky peak
70 Three (comb. form)
72 The Way
73 Aged
74 Legume

✦ Moored Homonyms ✦

ACROSS

1 Ana or Claus
6 High point
10 Yarn
14 Pricker
15 Pancake shop
16 Earthenware crock (Spanish)
17 Fuming
18 Rank
19 Irani currency
20 Believing in more than one God
23 Commercials, for short
26 Italian river
27 Nuns
28 True dance?
31 Stitch up
32 Press
33 Uproariously
38 Part of QED
39 Devout
40 South Korean president
41 Retaliatory discourager
43 Of Earth's largest continent
44 Old Olds
45 Most sugary

47 Georgia's capital
51 Middle Eastern country (abbr.)
52 First state (abbr.)
53 Superior wagerer?
56 Suffix with "import" and "reluct"
57 Dillseed
58 Card and chit game
62 Groovy
63 Parrot's nostril area
64 Perfect
65 With thorough knowledge
66 Stepped on
67 Stop

DOWN

1 Missouri city's airport code
2 Tuna
3 Late month (abbr.)
4 Stumble
5 Small nation
6 Breezy eagle's nest?
7 Online activity
8 Clothes eaters
9 Swordsmen
10 Least favorite sausage?

11 Cream of the crop
12 Knack
13 Powders
21 Recline
22 Northern Italian lake
23 Carrying a weapon
24 Tractor maker
25 Egypt's Anwar
29 Well-read adverb
30 Big cats
34 Beat with cleverness
35 Drew back
36 Rent
37 Streisand musical
39 Lengthen

42 Descartes
43 Involving oxygen consumption
46 1970s awareness training (abbr.)
47 Adding apparatuses
48 Wooden joint part
49 Army officer (two words) (abbr.)
50 Baseball's Doubleday
54 Architect Saarinen
55 Astronaut Sally
59 Charitable arts org.
60 Car's need
61 Corrida shout

31

More
✕ Moored Homonyms ✕

ACROSS

1 Middle East resident
5 Naked animal? (with 5 DOWN)
9 Automaton
14 South African rope weapon
15 Sch.
16 Glue
17 Norse god
18 Immediately (abbr.)
19 Throat illness
20 Nastier
22 Headlong plunge
24 Compass point
25 Disinterested directors? (with 48 DOWN)
26 To this document, as in attached
28 Shier
30 Desert
34 German car (abbr.)
37 Not a hit
38 Childless nobleman? (with 61 ACROSS)
40 Facial hair
42 Former military member
43 Burt's friend, formally
44 Incorrect contraction
45 Rds.
46 Goodbye, with "for now" (two words)
47 Refrain
50 North or South
52 Raises
56 Emote
59 Stuff
60 Pager
61 See 38 ACROSS
63 City of Italia
65 Darn it!
66 Type of oil
67 Celine
68 Italian money
69 Winter toys
70 Past tense of do
71 Trees

DOWN

1 Cause of WWII explosion (two words)
2 Famous Beverly Hills drive
3 "Are you calling me _ ____?"
4 Outlawed group? (with 60 DOWN)
5 See 5 ACROSS
6 Lou Gehrig's disease (abbr.)
7 Beginners' textbooks
8 Nations under one ruler
9 Adjust again
10 Choose
11 Brought into life
12 Team animals
13 Use a keyboard
21 Swellings
23 Tropical American plant
26 Quiet
27 Billy goats' nemesis
29 Error
31 Hockey's Bobby, and family
32 Tired vegetable, with 34 DOWN
33 Places to stay
34 See 32 DOWN
35 Breckenridge
36 Past tense of go
39 Clothing
41 Guide
42 CV or resume
44 Star-shaped
48 See 25 ACROSS
49 Haystack find
51 Jane Fonda movie, with "of God"
53 Spring month
54 Equip with weapons again
55 Spanish girls (abbr.)
56 Learning letters
57 Jung or Sandberg
58 Straight
60 See 4 DOWN
62 Queer
64 Me, to Henri

32

✗ Entertaining Awards ✗

ACROSS

1 Gestation place
5 Theater award
9 Literature award
14 Away from the wind
15 Largest continent
16 Pavarotti specialty
17 Wealthy
18 In theory
20 Native American tribe or haircut
22 Verb forms
23 Beer
24 Old Exxon
27 Fiction award
31 Half of a fly
34 The Greatest
35 Auto accessory
36 Perform
37 Extinct bird
38 Anger
39 Pale
41 Savings account (abbr.)
42 European country
43 Flaxlike plant
45 Carry
46 Snakelike fish
47 Film award (two words)
50 French city
51 Poetic contraction
52 Consuming
57 Music award
60 From then on
64 Challenge
65 Film award
66 Kansas town
67 Paradise
68 Barely won, with "out"
69 TV award
70 1981 Oscar-winning Beatty film

DOWN

1 Heat up
2 Medley
3 Relating to machines
4 As an agent for, with "on" and "of"
5 Duty
6 Buckeye school (abbr.)
7 Little bite
8 Little bark
9 Proboscis
10 Ready for business
11 Sleeping places
12 Writer Stanley Gardner
13 Potato chip brand
19 Native American dialect
21 Causing fatigue
24 Aged

25 Word with "snow" or "water"
26 Frosty and friends
27 Split up and analyze
28 Run away to marry
29 Egypt-Syria union (abbr.)
30 One who goes back on a promise
31 Custom built
32 Clean by rubbing
33 French stage or German floor
40 Scots own
44 Fuss

48 Gymnast Korbut
49 Guide
52 British school
53 Japanese exclamation (two words)
54 Computer geeks, without an "h"
55 Dies ____ (Latin)
56 Socially-inept studier
57 Neither black nor white
58 TV's talking horse (two words)
59 Hankerings
61 Giant's word
62 Male turkey
63 Tree

33

✕ Pot of Gold ✕

ACROSS

1 Rainbow color
5 Aaron or Raymond
9 Tunes
14 Flat-topped hill
15 Philippine buffalo
16 The Little Mermaid
17 Word with "down" and "out"
18 Pitcher Wilhelm
19 Like a certain alcoholic beverage
20 Boob tubes (abbr.)
22 Rainbow color
24 Japanese delicacy
27 Israeli statesman Abba
28 Emit light
32 Auto accessory
33 Moral weakness
34 Soften
35 Oxford college
36 All possible
38 Ale house
39 Rainbow color
41 Famous word book (abbr.)
43 Economic measure
46 Swap
50 Speech defects
54 Abominable snowman
56 Sector
57 Bodies of water
58 Groan
59 Sail holder
60 Leaves out
61 Gave out cards
63 For tea
64 Arrow shooter
67 Spot
69 Nothing, to Juan
73 Mental picture
74 Town in Oklahoma
75 Percussion instrument
76 Cook's clothing protector
77 Yeses
78 Highlander

DOWN

1 German car (abbr.)
2 Southern general
3 Star-spangled country (abbr.)
4 More suggestive of nature
5 Scrooge's words
6 One, in Spanish
7 Rainbow colors (abbr.)
8 Atkinson-Cleese-Goldberg film (two words)
9 Identical
10 Rainbow color
11 Zero
12 Obtain
13 Foxy
21 Rainbow color
23 January, to Paco
24 Sold out (abbr.)
25 Former Egypt and Syria union (abbr.)
26 Star Wars (abbr.)
27 First woman
29 Length of pool
30 OH or OK school (abbr.)
31 Internet
37 Rainbow color
40 Serious story
42 A girl's best friend
43 Workout locale
44 New (prefix)
45 School org.
47 Giant lake near Uzbekistan
48 Fate
49 Consume
51 Snow runner
52 Owned animal
53 Draft agency (abbr.)
55 Rainbow color
62 Utopian garden
63 Kennedy and Turner
64 Secret org.
65 Ref
66 Average
68 Cravat
70 Rainbow part
71 Twosome
72 Qty.

34

Original Evil Spirits

ACROSS
1 Jai ____
5 Farming (prefix)
9 Dense clumps
14 *The Merry Widow* composer
15 Passed on
16 Get used to something unpleasant (variant)
17 Start of JFK's famous Berlin line, in English (three words)
18 Angel, in France
19 Restaurant listings
20 Dutch evil spirit?
22 Courses of frenzied behavior
24 Populous nation
25 Shooting star
26 Seen
28 Swelling
32 Flow's partner
35 Pots' partners
36 Spain's region
38 Evil spirits in cigarette form?
40 Prison CEOs
41 Rubs around
42 NY Congresswoman Lowey
43 Bean
44 Deserve
45 Nastiest
48 Street
50 Blockaded attack
54 Accessory for evil spirits?

57 Baby swan
58 Weighty
59 Aviation prefix
61 Dame
62 Running spot
63 French person
64 Underground plant part
65 Mexican dip
66 Object of Salinger's love and squalor
67 Spanish ladies, abbr.

DOWN
1 Excuse
2 Gain knowledge
3 Rashad
4 Middle Eastern people
5 This makes quite a difference (two words)
6 Dutch evil spirit (or rummy)?
7 Disappointments
8 Conceive
9 Timing
10 Awarded in error
11 Chinese name
12 Factual
13 Working meeting (abbr.)

21 Finely dressed
23 Resolve a conflict
25 Big hills (abbr.)
27 Rowers
29 Mineral finds
30 Fred's dinosaur
31 Simple
32 Scottish and/or Irish language group
33 Temple locale
34 Neolithic evil spirit?
37 Cheap and showy
39 Zealots
40 Ancient evil spirit?

42 Stomach upsets
46 Interlock
47 Big cats
49 Russian evil spirit?
51 Star Wars planet
52 City in Italia
53 French states
54 Adherents (suffix)
55 Zeus' daughter
56 Israeli airline
57 Porter or slaw
60 Evil spirit of the West Indies?

✕ Day Starters ✕

ACROSS
1 Liquid day starter
6 Recedes
10 Groups (abbr.)
14 Homer's tale
15 Hooray
16 Indonesian island
17 Human
18 Differ- or exist- ending
19 "I think _ ___ ..."
20 Fool (slang)
22 Emulating Plato
24 Cleopatra biter
27 Outer (prefix)
28 Common soccer score
29 Top card, and bottom
30 Spotted songbirds
33 Tale
35 Crunchy day starter
36 Wake-up day starter
38 Abominable snowman
39 Hollow musical instruments
40 Arab chieftain (variant)
44 Woozy feeling
46 Whispered comment
47 Book units
49 Surprises
51 TV alien
52 Tear
54 One to Nero (fem.)
55 Katherine, to friends
56 Baked day starters
58 Stiff-legged
60 French day starter?
61 Jane
63 Quartz or marble
67 Fat
68 Read with a laser
69 Frozen hut
70 Trees
71 Closed
72 Cable channel

DOWN
1 Sail
2 Little one (suffix)
3 Three, in ancient Rome
4 Soup containers
5 Most trendsetting
6 Glasses
7 There's a Big one in London
8 Meaty day starter
9 Lawmen
10 Death notice, for short
11 According to ethnic origin
12 Quick look
13 Burn lightly
21 Speed measure (abbr.)
23 Wings
24 Lawyer (abbr.)
25 Foot covering
26 Buttocks (British slang)
31 Utilizing
32 Shoe bottoms
34 Beauty's love
37 Gassy
39 Commercial dealings
41 White day starter
42 Concept
43 Remaining
45 Advanced Environmental Research, Inc. (abbr.)
46 Semetic language
47 Multiple
48 Acknowledge
50 Collection that reflects the character of something
51 Walk along
53 College subj. (abbr.)
57 Government agents, slang
59 Scrambled day starters
62 Doug of the LA Dodgers (1970s pitcher)
64 European peak
65 Fit exactly, with "tee" (two words)
66 Two or more eras

36

Portals

ACROSS

1   "Electric" rock group
5   Entrance, with 10 ACROSS
10 Hinged portal
14 En-lai
15 Juliet's beau
16 Edison's A.
17 Violent outbreak
18 Relating to birds
19 Northern state (abbr.)
20 As to (two words)
21 Washington's subway
22 Floor covering
23 Speck
24 Ship's dining hall
25 Golfer's need
26 Precious metal (Spanish)
28 Consumed
30 Internal, with 10 ACROSS
32 Pressed apples
34 Spell
35 Poem
36 What rose from the bleachers upon Casey's first strike (two words)
37 Chew and swallow
38 Currently
39 Pauls (Italian)
40 Treats badly
42 Specified periods of time
43 Target projectile
44 Alternative (Spanish)
47 Car's home entrance, with 10 ACROSS
51 Thinking body part
55 External, with 10 ACROSS
57 Seventh Zodiac sign
58 Speak angrily
59 Vehicles
61 Club payments
62 Teen worry
63 Replacement
64 This or east (Spanish)
65 Group of players
66 Groups of animals
67 Cold water mammal

DOWN

1   Bitter
2   Cotton pants fabric
3   Premium delivery
4   Delightfully pretty
5   Surround
6   Roams
7   Leaves out
8   Close to
9   Wildly enjoyable, with "fun" (slang)
10 Inferno author
11 A goodie
12 Roundish
13 Leaf scraper
24 Famous "Portals" member
25 The feel of a surface
27 Kingdom
28 In front
29 Sack with special leaves
30 Wedding vows (two words)
31 Recent; unused
32 Mil. Officer (abbr.)
33 Day of wrath, dies ____
35 U2 song
41 Walking steps
45 Specific path
46 Word with space
48 The result of 40 ACROSS
49 Garbo
50 Artist's stand
51 Spoiled child
52 Speed contest
53 The King of Siam's companion
54 Unit
56 Frog's cousin
59 Bat material
60 '60s radical org. (abbr.)

37

✦ Colorful Rhymes ✦

ACROSS

1 Lofty
5 Daisy
10 Student's concern (abbr.)
13 Wrong
14 Colorful Arctic rhyme, with 64 ACROSS
15 Homonym for the first half of 15 DOWN
16 Where this puzzle's theme words might appear
17 Targeted
18 Tilt
19 Belgian salad leaf
21 Scares
23 Personal
25 Hwys.
26 Ties, as in a score
27 Palm off
28 Atmospheric, combining form
29 British cars, for short
30 Smelly (variant)
32 Seed holder
33 Dan on *Bonanza*
37 French Allen
38 Advanced teaching degree (abbr.)
39 Traditional Japanese gates
40 Singer Loretta
41 Wager
42 Weeding with a certain tool
43 Kublai or Chaka
45 Looked at
46 Chicle
47 French port city
49 Leg bone
50 Biblical abbr.
51 Warnings
52 Human
54 Cover uniformly
55 California county
57 See 47 DOWN
60 Russian missile used by Iraq
61 Similar
62 Basket game
63 Squeeze by
64 See 14 ACROSS
65 Common contraction

DOWN

1 Occurence
2 WWII island battle, with "Jima"
3 Colorful vegetable rhyme
4 Solemn song
5 Looked forward to
6 Shake from cold
7 New York and London paper
8 French summer
9 Colorful hairy rhyme
10 Astronaut/senator
11 Fertilizing mosses
12 Grass parts
15 Colorful footwear rhyme
20 Gradually deplete
22 Mean, median or mode (abbr.)
23 Unused parts of a butchered animal
24 Lawless, with "wild" (variant)
29 Boy's name
31 Fiddled around with
32 Tap
34 Master copies
35 Nasal passage
36 18th Greek letter
38 "Grown-up" boys
39 Small cities
41 Cricket player
42 Cook's sanitary headgear
44 Pres. before DDE
45 An Arab ruler
47 Card game, with 57 ACROSS
48 Variety show
49 Small plant shoot
51 Church part
53 California town
56 Latter-day Clay
58 Capable of
59 Set of articles or tools

⭑ Geometric Homonyms ⭑

ACROSS

1 Part of Rat Race's predecessor (two words)
5 Paine's Common
10 Not us
14 Moniker
15 Where Spain's rain falls
16 Prefix with "nautic" and "dynamic"
17 Dines
18 Modesty
20 Ruined spaces between two lines that meet? (with 21 ACROSS)
21 See 20 ACROSS
22 The Emerald Isle
23 Sleep state
25 Non-metallic element in a binary compound (suffix)
26 Add more troops (variant)
29 Light gas
33 Three (prefix)
34 Tree juice
36 Copy onto a cassette
37 Title for a man who gathers selectively? (with 51 ACROSS)
40 Football RB's stat (abbr.)
42 Spigot
44 Hwy.
45 Scores well on a test
47 Drink slowly
49 Vicious
51 See 37 ACROSS

52 Felons' outdoor sleeping shelters? (two words)
57 Automotive group (abbr.)
60 Depression
61 "__ _ penny, pick it up..."
62 Similar chemical substance
65 Jointly endorses?
66 Female sibling through marriage
69 Explorer John, et al.
70 A type of ranger
71 Lift a glass
72 Suffix with "kitchen"
73 Creature with no legs
74 Freeway egresses
75 Meeting in court (abbr.)

DOWN

1 Provide a solution
2 Maurice, informally
3 Amp, formally
4 Lineage
5 Figures that resemble orbs
6 The one that got away
7 War locale, for short
8 Brother or sister, for short
9 Chou
10 Bronzed man?
11 Command to Fido
12 Gaelic

13 Spanish branch hugger
19 Finish
24 Masters of Ceremonies (abbr.)
27 Dip in hot oil
28 Consume
30 Hearing part
31 Choose
32 Originally called
35 Travel documents
37 End of cul
38 Hospital area (abbr.)
39 Family member (abbr.)
41 Mistaken in the original
43 Pendulum's partner

46 Slouched
48 School of dolphins
50 Wants
53 Most friendly
54 Make useless
55 True doctrines
56 Talks back to
58 Ad agency client managers
59 Correspond
62 CA town, with "Vista"
63 Cease
64 The goddess of wine
67 White or Red
68 Drink, with mai

Armchair Puzzlers • Crosswords

✕ 2nd Grade Homonyms ✕

ACROSS

1 Pekoe
4 Dangerous
10 Learning place (abbr.)
13 Height (abbr.)
14 Idea
15 Homonym #1
16 French girl (abbr.)
17 Evil acts
18 Once more
19 Peacock or peahen
21 Landed property
23 Airport level, sometimes
25 Fit within
26 Napoleonic marshal
27 Homonym #2
29 Broadcasting (two words)
32 Type of slide
37 These are last in 32 ACROSS
38 Variant of riata
39 Ballet dress
40 Ancestors
42 Homonym #2
43 Land measure
44 Long, wide creek
45 Homonym #3
49 Umbrella companion
54 Hoagies, subs or grinders
55 King or queen
56 Oklahoma town
57 Legislative body
60 Fish eggs
61 South American empire
62 Spring holiday
63 Flawed clothing (abbr.)
64 Dorm leaders
65 Steps
66 Compass direction

DOWN

1 2003 Super Bowl winner
2 Fudd
3 Hot streak, in baseball (two words)
4 Reveal
5 Scandinavian nation
6 Not moving
7 Goal
8 Opponent
9 Mexican town
10 French 57 ACROSS
11 Mediterranean island
12 Struck with an axe
15 Toppers
20 With limits
22 Servant attached to the land
24 Curser
28 Diner sign
29 Not on
30 New (prefix)
31 Atmospheric prefix
32 Homonym #1
33 New York college town
34 Mourn
35 Stanza (abbr.)
36 Mon. follower (abbr.)
38 Indentations
41 Naked
42 Victors
44 Rabblerouser
45 Homonym #3
46 Hair dye
47 Clapton and others
48 *Star Wars* character
50 Nicolo's violin
51 Senator Hatch
52 Oak fruit
53 Homonym #3
58 Consume food
59 Secret org. (abbr.)

40

✕ Bonds ✕

ACROSS

1. WWI plane
5. Pear
9. Bond
14. Sunblock ingredient (abbr.)
15. Margarine
16. Nebraska city
17. Gem
18. Dudley's gal
19. Religious ceremonies
20. Steal cattle
22. Dark horse
24. California lake
25. Population count
26. Low point
28. Pretends
32. Lyric poem
35. Soaks, as in flax
36. Cookie
37. Bond, by George
39. Bond
42. Lists of corrections
43. Young one
44. Indian state or Tibetan gazelle
45. Pesky biting fly
46. Library study area
48. ET's friend
50. Welles or Bean
55. Obstructions
58. Involuntary expulsion of air
59. Skip
60. Org. (abbr.)
62. Noah's numbers
63. Writes down
64. Moniker
65. Lease
66. Sheep
67. African antelopes
68. Mineral sources

DOWN

1. Athletic game
2. World's second largest island
3. To make uneasy
4. Bond
5. Skeleton piece
6. Spanish exclamation
7. Bond
8. Punctuation mark
9. Place for bodies
10. Mistake by neglect
11. Vow
12. Current or flow (prefix)
13. Compass point
21. Past participle of learn
23. Science org. (abbr.)
25. Metropolis
27. Sudden collapse
29. Brady or LeMond
30. Roman fiddler
31. Legume
32. Designer Cassini
33. Mend socks
34. Book of the Bible
38. Diners
39. It goes after the horse
40. British award (abbr.)
41. Synthetic fabric
43. 007 portrayer
47. Broadcasting
49. Covers
51. Fashion based on the past
52. Underground pipe for waste
53. Protective layer
54. Birds' homes
55. Persistent annoyance
56. Declare
57. Memorization
58. Fancy hotel rooms (abbr.)
61. Dallas college (abbr.)

41

✦ Night-Night ✦

ACROSS
1 Nocturnal activity
6 Nocturnal activity
11 Not as old
12 Jack Sprat did this to fat (two words)
13 Adjective for nocturnal counting animal
14 Salem victim
15 Stimpy's friend
16 Currency of Myanmar
19 Fortune teller
20 Unit of work or energy
21 After "ars"
23 When nocturnal activities happen
25 Loiter
28 Where nocturnal activities happen
31 Hitler
32 Accustom
34 Zellweger
35 Land measures
36 Language (suffix)
37 Inflated language
40 Snouts
41 These hold heads during nocturnal activities
45 These clothe bodies during nocturnal activities (abbr.)
48 Thought
49 One of seven
51 Ingest
52 To draw out
54 Hang with cloth
56 Light amplification by stimulated emission of radiation (abbr.)
57 Type of parrot
58 Conveyances with runners
59 British guns

DOWN
1 Nocturnal sound
2 Switch
3 Patrick of basketball
4 Poetic contraction
5 Type of school, for short
6 Nocturnal product of Mother Nature
7 Lift
8 Small (plural suffix)
9 Action or process (suffix)
10 "Silent Night, Holy Night" author
17 Safecracker
18 Arthur of tennis
22 Mark with fine grooves
23 World's longest river
24 Dante's hell
25 With 23 ACROSS, making 6 ACROSS scary
26 Summer drinks
27 Solo
28 Hamilton's duel opponent
29 Part of Elba palindrome (two words)
30 Portrayal (abbr.)
33 CPOs, e.g.
38 Whys companions
39 To be (Latin)
41 Medicinal tablets
42 Perfect
43 Rent
44 Tied up (shoes)
45 State of harmony
46 Asian island nation
47 Cooks by simmering
50 Naval big guns (abbr.)
53 Bonds hit 73 (abbr.)
55 Mouse's cousin

42

✕ All Good Things ✕

ACROSS

1 Written mistake
5 Aides (abbr.)
10 Watch chain or pocket
13 Earth follower
14 Retail outlet
15 The Wizard of 24 DOWN, middle name
16 Soon
17 Region of New Guinea
18 Small pierced piece for a necklace
19 This puzzle's theme
21 This puzzle's theme
23 Unit of linguistic structure (suffix)
25 *Exodus* author Leon
26 Yoko
27 ___ Miserables
28 Insult (slang)
29 Force
32 Lowest-ranking USN officer
34 What all good things must come to
35 Big Sky State (abbr.)
37 This puzzle's theme
38 Cook's need
39 Stringed instrument
40 Act addressed by a civil suit
41 Vehicle
42 Atlanta bird
43 Feels pain
45 Repeat a passage, in music
46 Soap base
47 Confidence game
49 Columbian city
50 Naval abbr.
51 European plane
52 Lanes
54 Birthright holder
55 Father's brother
57 Affected manners meant to impress
60 Rock's companion
61 Helicopter blade
62 Pillage
63 Offs antonym
64 Revises
65 Plural version of theme

DOWN

1 Extinct airline
2 Distant, but visible
3 College teacher
4 All (prefix)
5 Pain killer
6 Stoppage
7 Second yr. students (abbr.)
8 Toy chain (abbr.)
9 Edible fish
10 Leaping parasite
11 Elliptical
12 Past tense of bid
15 Unusual
20 Give a little push
22 Resembling (suffix)
23 Choose
24 First word of NJ or CA town
29 News channel
30 This puzzle's theme
31 Gets pleasure from
33 Not Constantinople
34 Hearing organ
36 Shades of color
38 Step or dance
39 Famous Count
41 This puzzle's theme
42 Things added to enlarge
44 Hospital section (abbr.)
45 List of candidates
47 Buffalo
48 Europe-Asia dividers
49 Sharp-pointed plants
51 Aircraft, combining form
53 Ivy League school
56 Doze, with "off"
58 Fishing pole
59 Sad to say (IM abbr.)

43

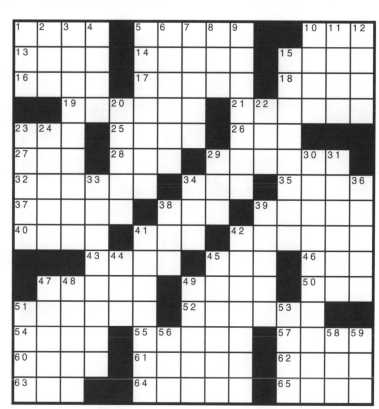

✗ Bad Jokes ✗

ACROSS

1 Western state
5 March time
9 Bad joke subject
14 Prefix for one million
15 Empty set
16 Tennessee politician, to friends
17 Prefix for equal
18 Of the, in France (two words)
19 Grossly overweight
20 Physicist Schrödinger
22 Part of a bad joke pair, with 59A
24 State of matter
25 Bad joke subject
28 Conceptions of perfection
30 Dwight's wife
31 Flyboys
33 Can follower
35 Rhyming tie follower
36 Game sequence
40 Can preceder
41 Bad joke subjects
44 *Matrix* character
45 Biblical character, with "er"
47 Windy City (abbr.)
48 Native American chief
50 Japanese, for example
53 Forbidden dog?
54 Capers
57 Told tales
59 Part of a bad joke pair, with 22A
60 Govt. financial agency (abbr.)
62 34D fighter (abbr.)
63 Tear-jerking veggie
65 Part of a bad joke pair, with 49D
67 Scottish skirt
70 Aunt's partner
71 Tiny amount
72 Author Wiesel
73 Toddlers
74 This' partner
75 9/11 heroes (abbr.)

DOWN

1 Baseball ref
2 Boston Party subject
3 Consensus
4 180° turn
5 Home for one billion 50A
6 Chaperon
7 Printer's measure
8 Grand follower
9 9A + e
10 Test site, for short
11 Greek letter
12 Of the nose
13 Legless garment
21 Car part
23 Pointers
25 Express emotion, theatrically
26 Blue stone
27 Cleaning, with "up"
29 Medical specialty (abbr.)
32 Bread seed
34 Colorful discrimination
37 Not a fairy-tale ending
38 Della or Pee Wee
39 Wanderer
42 NHL merger grp. (abbr.)
43 Spicy music?
46 Shark (German)
49 Part of a bad joke pair, with 65A
51 Biscuit-like pastries
52 Musical composition
54 Regarding
55 Governess/babysitter
56 Treat's partner
58 Anwar
61 Limey
64 Opry preceder
66 Aah's companion
68 Mouth surrounder
69 Kennedy, to friends

44

✕ Horsin' Around ✕

ACROSS

1 Untrue
6 Accumulated knowledge
10 Software command
14 Salty compound
15 Tennis score (two words)
16 Hi-tech modeling process
17 Book promo line
18 King follower
19 Attila
20 Spuds
22 Regarding
23 Attain with great effort, with "out"
26 Steal
27 Extensive enterprises
29 Design with letters
32 Vehicle stopper (abbr.)
33 Polo
34 Spiritual guide
36 Advanced toward
40 African plant
41 Danger
42 Coll. (abbr.)
43 Hall, in Mazatlan
44 Eastern European native
45 From then until now
46 Digits (abbr.)
48 90 degree maneuver (two words)
50 Stir up
54 Batter's stat (abbr.)
55 Man with a salty wife
56 Fortunetelling cards
57 Song words

60 Greek marketplace
61 Egyptian queen, informally
62 Asian nation on a peninsula
66 Longest geologic time periods
67 Window ledge
68 Formal command
69 Aide (abbr.)
70 Apple shooter William
71 Stove

DOWN

1 Winter mo. (abbr.)
2 Sci. inst. (abbr.)
3 Baton Rouge school (abbr.)
4 Separate by type
5 Trade ban
6 A water-bread horse? (two words)
7 Smell
8 Wash with water
9 Sch. subj. (abbr.)
10 Famous movie waterbread horse
11 Movie star
12 Principle or standard
13 Corrects and adapts
21 High crag

22 Police search tool (abbr.)
23 Bovary and Peel
24 Eucalyptus-eating Australian mammal
25 Register (var.)
28 Injure by beating
30 Another waterbread horse? (two words)
31 Wall painting
35 Another waterbread horse? (two words)
37 Declare invalid
38 Small-scale
39 Occurrence
41 Inconspicuous interjection

45 Adhesive label
47 Edible grain
49 Govt. det. agency (abbr.)
50 Not in port (two words)
51 Cats, to Jose
52 Golf clubs
53 *Phantom Menace* princess
58 Scream
59 Pop
61 Time zone (abbr.)
63 Word before Tin-Tin
64 Heart diagnosis machine (abbr.)
65 Absorbed as food

45

✶ Snappy Comebacks ✶

ACROSS

1 First part of comebacks
5 Little Red Hen's words
9 With 1A and 48D, comeback to "Would he hurry up already?"
14 The Pequod's captain
15 Behold what was born this day (two words)
16 Country of ink?
17 Second starter
18 Light or tulip follower
19 Bike part
20 Long-necked wading birds
22 Angry
24 Compass dir. (abbr.)
25 Lessened pain
26 Bodies at rest tend to stay ____ ____
28 Tubes for transferring liquid
30 Sparkling Italian city?
34 Mid. Eastern nation (abbr.)
37 Floating marker
38 Beans or small cars
40 With 1A and 48D, comeback to "Surely you jest!"
42 A villain to 2D
43 Simpler
44 Skin or throw
45 Sandwich (abbr.)
46 First garden
47 Frozen dripping water
50 Soviet forced labor camps
52 With 1A and 48D, comeback to "Roger, over and out."
56 Summary, with "in a"
59 What she's come, to the Guess Who
60 For want of this, the rider was lost (two words)
61 Jet king?
63 Tiny amount
64 Chinese mammal
65 Tall hills (abbr.)
66 Previously owned
67 Western German city
68 This, to Pablo
69 No more than specified

DOWN

1 Tango, for example
2 Gotham's chief
3 Grandmas
4 Steaks
5 Snatches
6 Buckeye or Cowboy
7 Russian literary giant
8 Possessed at birth
9 Rubs dry
10 Homonym for won
11 Horse race numbers
12 Portuguese navigator Bartolomeu
13 Ivy League school
21 Fit for use as food
23 Say letters in order again
26 Nautical cry
27 Astronaut's drink
29 Childish
31 Accidentally bump into, toe first
32 Work
33 Common contraction
34 Words of understanding
35 Roe producer
36 Increase, as in prices
39 Rookie doctor
41 Real "box" seats
42 Muscles, for short
44 Young porcine animals
48 Second part of comebacks (two words)
49 Na
51 Polish horse cavalry member
53 Migratory bird
54 Go into
55 Book consumer, minus an "r"
56 Neck part
57 A few, to Juan
58 Treats with tannic acid
59 Major or Minor
62 Hill inhabitant

46

✶ The Twain Shall Meet ✶

ACROSS

1 Tree-free grassy plain
6 Hoist
10 Kitchen measures (abbr.)
14 Resell at a higher price
15 90° bends
16 Greek queen of the gods
17 Examine closely
18 Wings
19 Middle of QED
20 Holey sifters
22 Tart or sharp
23 Consciousness-raising seminar
26 Corrida shout
27 Half of where Mark Twain wanted to end up, with 30D (two words)
29 Zero-ed out particle
32 Plane's speedometer (abbr.)
33 New Indian city
34 Excessively flattering
37 Return mail device (abbr.)
38 A famous riveter
39 Blue color
42 Affirms
44 A complete 180
45 WWII govt. agency that regulated prices (abbr.)
46 The Flintstones' time period (two words)
48 Musical show
52 Keyboard key (abbr.)
53 Kareem before he was Kareem

54 Stay away from
55 Pay to free
58 FDR's coin
59 Miriam's nickname
60 Asp
64 Irritating little flyer
65 Mild epithet
66 Run away to wed
67 First word of a children's rhyme used for making a choice
68 Trudge
69 Decorated again

DOWN

1 Messages added to the ends of letters (abbr.)
2 College conference known for great hoops teams (abbr.)
3 Chinese leader
4 In addition to
5 Deductive (two words)
6 The other half of where Twain wanted to end up, with 10D
7 Fashion magazine
8 Hero Gordon
9 3D follower
10 The other half of where Twain wanted to end up, with 6D
11 Font creature
12 Madrid museum
13 Woodland creature

21 Biblical judge
22 Too
23 Finishes
24 "___ _ penny, pick it up . . ."
25 OK city
28 Where it's "at", for soldiers
30 Half of where Mark Twain wanted to end up, with 27A
31 Ejects
35 Using one's ears
36 Identical amount
38 Raise, as in children
40 Strongly suggest
41 All over again
43 Raced

44 Find and reveal
47 WWII spy agency (abbr.)
48 Get by begging
49 Sheep adjective
50 Donne's famous starter (two words)
51 Test under pressure, with "by fire"
56 Bullets, for short
57 Distance
59 Doctors (abbr.)
61 Ultra-cool MP3 player, with "i"
62 Faulty word, with "center"
63 Primary color

47

Armchair Puzzlers · Crosswords

Why?

ACROSS

1 Old TV comedy, with "Smart"
4 Vomit
8 Organ
13 Lge. rds. (abbr.)
15 Geometric expanse
16 French city
17 With 60A, driving place?
18 Farmer's place
19 Half of a Washington city
20 Of the country
22 Korean car
24 Ending with "command" and "musket"
25 A word that should be spelled like it sounds?
28 SF or NY sports team
30 Songbirds
31 2003 World Series victor
33 "Crat" starter
35 Word with Paolo
36 Narcotic
40 Possessive pronoun
41 Repeats
44 Govt. org. (abbr.)
45 Non-permanent worker, for short
47 Soldier or sailor (abbr.)
48 Transcribers, for short
50 Foot or shoe part
53 Cooking devices
54 Cooking devices
57 Parking place?
59 Summer drink
60 With 17A, driving place?
62 Symphony with song
63 Swell
65 Ms. Bovary
67 Flows' partner
70 Game that ends with a shout
71 Devices that make elec. guitars louder
72 Slimy crawler
73 Norwegian playwright
74 Soaks
75 Outdoor shelter

DOWN

1 Clothing retailer
2 Peron or Gabor
3 Security concern
4 Former Egyptian president
5 Qualifier, for short
6 Slithery swimmer
7 Q: What do you call a fly without wings? A: A ___
8 State that shouldn't have interstates, but does
9 Time period
10 Comedian Steve
11 Rent again
12 Russian kings
14 Pepe Le Pew and friends
21 Remainder
23 Frozen houses
25 Braid
26 Author Brett
27 Made a chess move
29 Run-on connector
32 Mouse's cousin
34 Black Sea port
37 Replaceable
38 Half of a fairy tale starter (two words)
39 Resembling a fossil fuel
42 Whole number (abbr.)
43 Cooking device
46 Poke inhabitant
49 The king of mountains
51 Man who understood the gravity of the situation
52 On time
54 Jewish teacher
55 Improvise (two words)
56 Sign gases
58 Bridge player's non-bid (two words)
61 2000, for one
64 Time period
66 French woman (abbr.)
68 Bread roll or hair roll
69 NCO (abbr.)

48

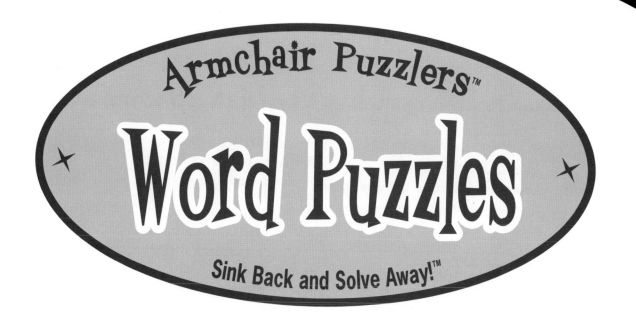

49

Word Puzzles: Instructions

Word Muddles
Unscramble each word related to a particular theme.

Before & After
Fill in the blanks to connect the names. Each blank will be the last name of the person before it and the first name of the person after it.

Letter Shuffle
Change just ONE letter in each word to create a new group of words that is linked by a common theme.

EXAMPLE:
dairy/nose/tarnation/lilt/penny

SOLUTION: TYPES OF FLOWERS
daisy/rose/carnation/lily/peony

Antonym Word Search
First unscramble the word and then find its antonym (opposite) hidden in the word search.

It Takes Two
Fill in the blanks to form words using the same two consonants for the entire puzzle.

Acrostics
Figure out the clues in Part 1, fill in the answers and transfer the letters to their corresponding numbers in Part 2.

When completed, Part 2 will be either a literary quote followed by the book title or a musical quote followed by the name of the song.

Answers to all Word Puzzles begin on page 191.

Animal Talk

drca kshra   _____ _____

iapbggkcy   _____

nnheimseoky   _____

lawkatc   _____

bdri aribn   _____ _____

aidrblji   _____

oohepinegl   _____

owikclc   _____

kcbal peseh   _____ _____

blulrdoez   _____

51

Al

_____

            _____

            Sassoon

Andy

_____

            _____

            Gable

52

LeTter •Shuffle•

Ell	Fin	Leech	Yak	Calm
_____	_____	_____	_____	_____

ANTONYM WORD SEARCH

L	N	E	D	D	I	H	A	I	L
S	E	O	D	R	M	L	A	C	S
X	V	R	A	I	S	T	D	J	T
U	A	B	R	I	G	H	T	O	M
H	E	U	I	A	P	I	F	L	O
G	R	P	E	L	O	X	R	L	R
S	U	O	I	V	B	O	Q	U	K
M	P	A	E	H	C	S	K	D	C
E	R	L	Y	R	A	E	B	N	A

PLEBAIL

IFLECA

OYRSMT

TOYLSC

BEIVLIS

NARDAIT

it

Takes

Two

BEFORE & AFTER

Ashley

_____

_____

Rockefeller

Jesse

_____

_____

Diaz

LeTter • Shuffle •

Pot	Mock	Soup	Sling	Clues

_____ _____ _____ _____ _____

ANTONYM WORD SEARCH

Y	R	E	T	S	Y	M	X	G	Y
X	O	A	J	X	A	S	M	N	N
D	T	S	S	I	M	E	R	I	G
E	N	I	E	L	C	D	W	V	J
V	W	O	U	D	R	L	D	I	O
A	O	L	A	G	U	R	F	G	E
U	N	P	F	I	U	R	S	H	B
S	K	C	O	M	Q	U	C	D	E
N	R	A	B	Y	K	C	U	L	N

NUBEAR

GEMANI

FURLACE

FIGYORL

DJXINE

TNGIYS

55

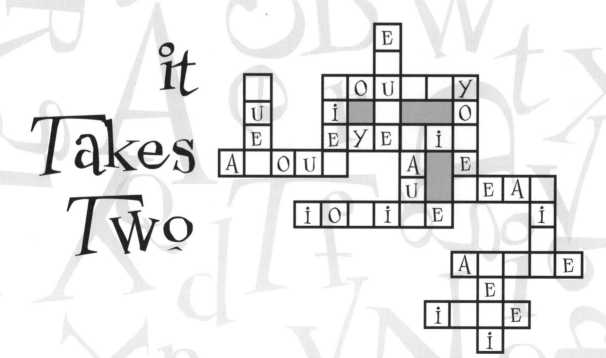

it

Takes

Two

ACROSTIC—PART 1

A) Extortionist

45	26	18	13	75	36	40	53	58

B) Pointy beard

65	30	3	48	38	14

C) Make teeth brighter

6	43	10	23	68	20

D) Clerk's job

16	31	63	24	78	52

E) Very smallest

9	70	51	17	34	64	11

F) Alice's dreamland

46	57	67	28	60	33	37	7	27	79

G) Writer

39	66	61	22	54	5	35	4

H) Subject of a Longfellow poem

74	41	12	76	50	25	2	19

I) From Stockholm

29	32	44	59	47	55	72

J) Dual

73	1	62	8

K) Early American party

69	49	77	21

L) Hue

42	15	56	71

56

ACROSTIC—PART 2
Literary Quote

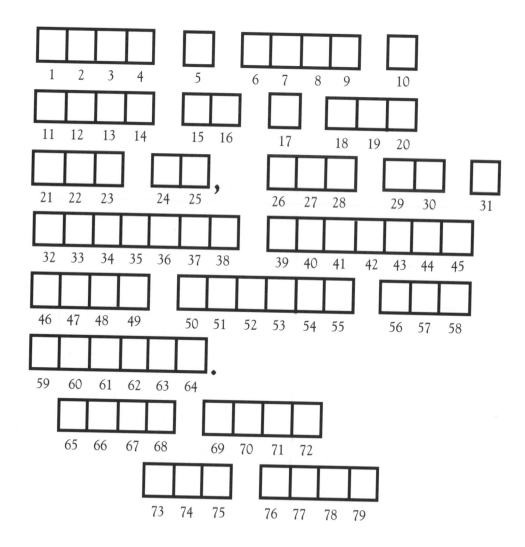

```
┌─┬─┬─┬─┐   ┌─┐   ┌─┬─┬─┬─┐   ┌─┐
│ │ │ │ │   │ │   │ │ │ │ │   │ │
└─┴─┴─┴─┘   └─┘   └─┴─┴─┴─┘   └─┘
 1  2  3  4    5     6  7  8  9   10
```

```
┌─┬─┬─┬─┐   ┌─┬─┐   ┌─┐   ┌─┬─┬─┐
│ │ │ │ │   │ │ │   │ │   │ │ │ │
└─┴─┴─┴─┘   └─┴─┘   └─┘   └─┴─┴─┘
11 12 13 14   15 16   17    18 19 20
```

```
┌─┬─┬─┐   ┌─┬─┐   ┌─┬─┬─┐   ┌─┬─┐   ┌─┐
│ │ │ │   │ │ │ , │ │ │ │   │ │ │   │ │
└─┴─┴─┘   └─┴─┘   └─┴─┴─┘   └─┴─┘   └─┘
21 22 23   24 25    26 27 28   29 30   31
```

```
┌─┬─┬─┬─┬─┬─┬─┐   ┌─┬─┬─┬─┬─┬─┬─┐
│ │ │ │ │ │ │ │   │ │ │ │ │ │ │ │
└─┴─┴─┴─┴─┴─┴─┘   └─┴─┴─┴─┴─┴─┴─┘
32 33 34 35 36 37 38   39 40 41 42 43 44 45
```

```
┌─┬─┬─┬─┐   ┌─┬─┬─┬─┬─┬─┐   ┌─┬─┬─┐
│ │ │ │ │   │ │ │ │ │ │ │   │ │ │ │
└─┴─┴─┴─┘   └─┴─┴─┴─┴─┴─┘   └─┴─┴─┘
46 47 48 49   50 51 52 53 54 55   56 57 58
```

```
┌─┬─┬─┬─┬─┬─┐
│ │ │ │ │ │ │ .
└─┴─┴─┴─┴─┴─┘
59 60 61 62 63 64
```

```
┌─┬─┬─┬─┐   ┌─┬─┬─┬─┐
│ │ │ │ │   │ │ │ │ │
└─┴─┴─┴─┘   └─┴─┴─┴─┘
65 66 67 68   69 70 71 72
```

```
┌─┬─┬─┐   ┌─┬─┬─┬─┐
│ │ │ │   │ │ │ │ │
└─┴─┴─┘   └─┴─┴─┴─┘
73 74 75   76 77 78 79
```

ACROSTIC—PART 1

A) Confuse or disorient

4	42	13	79	26	18	20	48

B) Front door

58	54	32	23	73	41	67	5

C) Married bliss

39	11	81	22	15	1	68	47	55

D) Boring

51	50	70	44	77	8	34

E) Like crops

49	66	12	65	37	29	33	62

F) Ancient Meso-American

76	61	43	28	17

G) Croaking amphibian

71	56	14	30

H) Pleasure vessel

3	59	24	72	35

I) Head start

25	9	21	31	69	60	16	10	75

J) Milk type

57	7	19	38	2	74

K) Looking jaundiced

6	36	63	27	40	46	64	45	52

L) A cereal grass

80	53	78

58

ACROSTIC—PART 2
Musical Quote

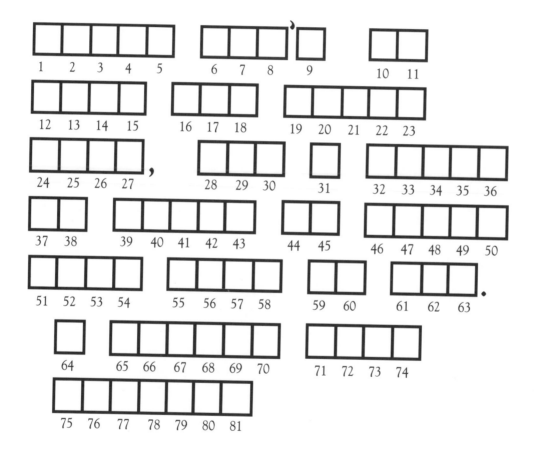

```
□□□□□   □□□'□   □□
1  2  3  4  5    6  7  8  9    10 11

□□□□   □□□   □□□□□
12 13 14 15   16 17 18   19 20 21 22 23

□□□□,   □□□   □   □□□□□
24 25 26 27    28 29 30   31   32 33 34 35 36

□□   □□□□□   □□   □□□□□
37 38   39 40 41 42 43   44 45   46 47 48 49 50

□□□□   □□□□   □□   □□□.
51 52 53 54   55 56 57 58   59 60   61 62 63

□   □□□□□□   □□□□
64   65 66 67 68 69 70   71 72 73 74

□□□□□□□
75 76 77 78 79 80 81
```

word muddles

Happy Campers

erfmaicp   _____

lssaawmhorlm   _____

kkcabcap   _____

hgfihsllat   _____

seomrs   _____

nrlnate   _____

eplnreetl   _____

itotle eprap   _____ _____

rltia ixm   _____ _____

pocsmas   _____

60

word muddles

Hot Lunch

ckciehn irnsfeg   ————— —————

trato stot   ————— —————

teolamfa   —————————

zpzai   —————————

gbesruecehre   —————————

ghspeitat   —————————

rdilegl seceeh   ————— —————

lgsaana   —————————

rongcsdo   —————————

altsaemlb   —————————

61

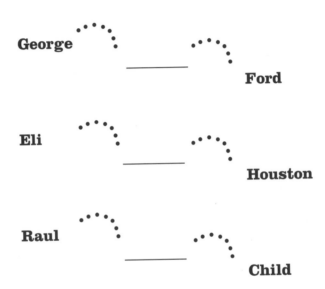

George .... ____ .... Ford

Eli .... ____ .... Houston

Raul .... ____ .... Child

62

LeTter • Shuffle •

Sing	Queer	Prance	Dupe	Mount
____	____	____	____	____

ANTONYM WORD SEARCH

O	T	S	U	G	S	I	D	G	Y
H	S	I	L	E	R	N	J	I	E
G	H	Z	P	L	A	I	N	N	T
U	S	H	G	X	Y	M	U	B	A
O	H	T	B	E	T	L	U	Q	H
R	O	U	D	I	J	O	L	T	D
M	W	R	T	S	D	P	R	N	L
V	Y	T	Y	A	L	S	I	M	E
A	R	L	C	F	U	I	Z	E	R

YESCATS

EVIBEEL

EDITCE

OHMSOT

CLEATO

HFALYS

63

it

Takes

Two

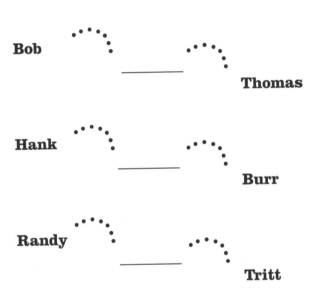

Bob   Thomas

Hank   Burr

Randy   Tritt

LeTter • Shuffle •

Steep   House   Pin   Loose   Roaster

_____   _____   _____   _____   _____

ANTONYM WORD SEARCH

P	R	E	I	T	O	L	X	C	V
E	S	D	T	P	M	O	R	P	O
R	A	C	B	A	F	F	I	R	M
S	E	U	I	P	C	E	Z	S	W
O	D	C	F	J	O	K	C	M	A
N	I	O	E	J	N	B	Y	I	G
A	L	A	Y	N	E	D	O	N	N
L	U	E	L	Y	T	S	R	I	E
S	Q	C	I	L	B	U	P	M	L

CANNITE

RTYDA

ANYTHUG

REVPITA

FOICRMN

SLAYCS

65

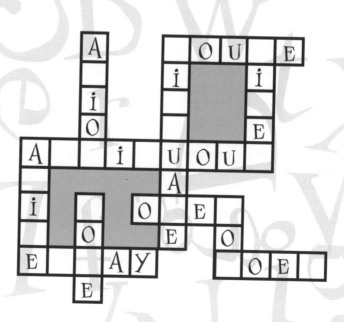

it
Takes
Two

Armchair Puzzlers • Word Puzzles

ACROSTIC—PART 1

A) A small crustacean

15	45	28	75	25	36	12	6

B) A lavish party

5	74	3	46	18	58	40	60

C) An omen

34	10	66	27	48	59	76	4	1

D) Potato pancake

64	22	70	30	14

E) A solemn toll

57	32	72	53	41

F) Bulbous onion

26	62	52	16	54	68	20

G) "White _____"

65	11	56	17	49	7	42	73

H) Sword case

77	21	19	47	61	71

I) Who's in charge

13	38	44	8

J) Least spoiled

69	37	63	43	51	35	50	23

K) Curtsied

55	29	39	2	67

L) Sharpen or hone

24	9	31	33

ACROSTIC—PART 2
Literary Quote

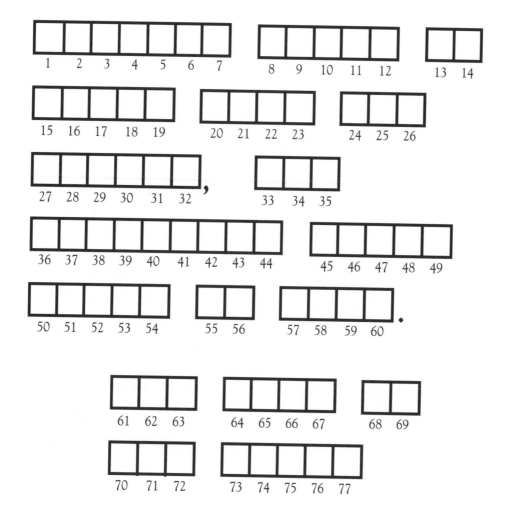

1	2	3	4	5	6	7

8	9	10	11	12

13	14

15	16	17	18	19

20	21	22	23

24	25	26

					|,
27	28	29	30	31	32

33	34	35

36	37	38	39	40	41	42	43	44

45	46	47	48	49

50	51	52	53	54

55	56

			|.
57	58	59	60

67

61	62	63

64	65	66	67

68	69

70	71	72

73	74	75	76	77

ACROSTIC—PART 1

A) Cuban dance

☐☐☐☐☐
4 63 31 36 16

B) Lawn guy

☐☐☐☐☐
27 6 2 24 54

C) Spotted scavenger

☐☐☐☐☐
13 42 35 58 69

D) Mode

☐☐☐☐☐☐☐
66 9 41 22 70 19 26

E) Paper cutter

☐☐☐☐☐☐☐☐
56 48 37 11 18 53 23 73

F) High esteem

☐☐☐☐☐
8 72 17 51 55

G) Veggie protein

☐☐☐☐
47 28 60 3

H) Animal life

☐☐☐☐☐
20 32 44 64 25

I) Email provider

☐☐☐☐☐
1 30 34 59 65

J) Rat on

☐☐☐☐☐☐
12 61 40 46 71 49

K) Bows

☐☐☐☐☐☐
68 45 62 15 39 7

L) Kiln

☐☐☐☐
43 67 33 21

M) A large shark

☐☐☐☐
29 5 10 57

N) Bar brew

☐☐☐☐
50 14 38 52

ACROSTIC—PART 2
Musical Quote

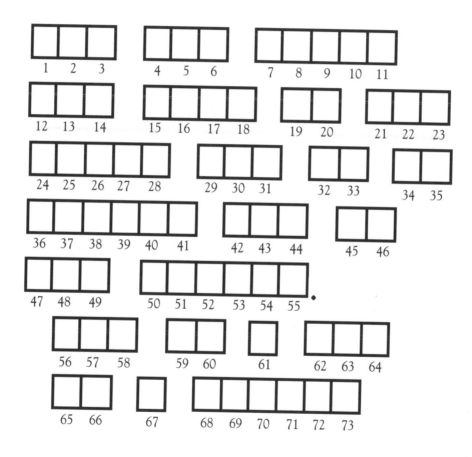

Anchors Away

taablosi   ———————————

baecarln   ———————————

cbnia   ———————————

pcaitan   ———————————

dinyhg   ———————————

yaellg   ———————————

oochesnr   ———————————

rcsyuv   ———————————

hytca   ———————————

ouagbtt   ———————————

70

word muddles

"C" Food Diet

arcosrt   _____

earlce   _____

radceem oncr   _____ _____

eaauochltp   _____

ekoioc   _____

udrstac   _____

prcee   _____

ecsresola   _____

roatnssic   _____

rclfiwluoae   _____

71

BEFORE & AFTER

Lenny

_____

_____

_____

Gaye

LeTteR •Shuffle•

Fear	Beer	Elm	Foe	Bagger
_____	_____	_____	_____	_____

ANTONYM WORD SEARCH

K	I	N	B	O	Y	B	M	N	J
U	R	I	F	T	R	X	T	Y	N
R	V	A	S	W	R	E	A	T	K
E	I	P	D	D	X	N	H	P	D
W	V	F	M	C	E	S	G	M	O
O	I	R	Y	I	D	L	H	E	O
L	D	U	L	G	W	C	L	N	S
N	E	A	Q	I	K	C	E	I	W
Z	T	C	E	S	L	A	F	P	F

CADROW

FLIPUT

DINKDER

HBGRIT

RETCROC

UCAUVSO

it

Takes

Two

Etta

_____

_____

_____

Sheen

LeTter • Shuffle •

Mop   Balk   Sink   Quick   Weigh

_____   _____   _____   _____   _____

ANTONYM WORD SEARCH

L	O	U	R	E	W	U	Y	A	U
R	I	A	F	E	L	J	T	D	E
M	E	I	N	L	T	E	I	U	Q
J	H	E	X	D	W	R	D	O	U
K	R	E	V	E	E	I	X	L	I
O	S	L	G	D	S	D	C	H	T
A	Q	D	E	A	Y	A	U	D	L
S	U	I	R	J	K	L	N	R	E
L	G	N	I	V	O	M	J	U	Y

IPLEOT

RIMGNAT

STNUJU

AECLNC

AVENI

SOYIN

it

Takes

Two

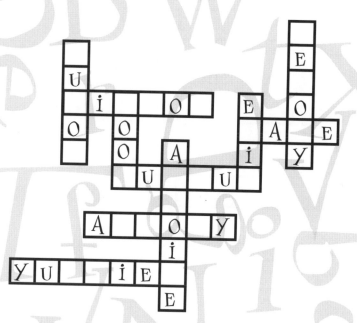

ACROSTIC—PART 1

A) A sheep's coat

88	29	94	76	65	59

B) Bahamas archipelago

33	90	52	37		17	44	22	53	39	99

C) Small stone shooter

73	19	40	92	93	54	2	10	74

D) Flightless African bird

27	64	1	31	77	60	26

E) Old Spanish gold

68	87	7	48	62	13	80	16

F) Twelve times a year

14	6	67	9	38	70	63

G) San Francisco's Fisherman's ___

43	45	69	96	28

H) Acid problem

75	98	49	81	82	89	46	57	84

I) Key in a murder trial

12	3	66	79	42	21

J) Broderick or Perry

78	95	100	35	36	15	25

K) Coin depository?

11	71	72	8	32	83	34	24

L) Windblown sea spray

47	55	91	97	51	41	30	58	61

M) Not a soul

50	20		23	18	86

N) The highest point

4	85	5	56

ACROSTIC—PART 2
Literary Quote

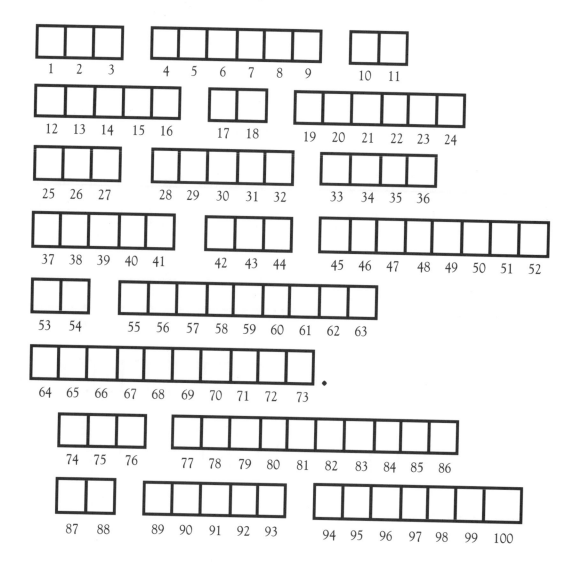

| 1 | 2 | 3 | | 4 | 5 | 6 | 7 | 8 | 9 | | 10 | 11 |

| 12 | 13 | 14 | 15 | 16 | | 17 | 18 | | 19 | 20 | 21 | 22 | 23 | 24 |

| 25 | 26 | 27 | | 28 | 29 | 30 | 31 | 32 | | 33 | 34 | 35 | 36 |

| 37 | 38 | 39 | 40 | 41 | | 42 | 43 | 44 | | 45 | 46 | 47 | 48 | 49 | 50 | 51 | 52 |

| 53 | 54 | | 55 | 56 | 57 | 58 | 59 | 60 | 61 | 62 | 63 |

| 64 | 65 | 66 | 67 | 68 | 69 | 70 | 71 | 72 | 73 | .

| 74 | 75 | 76 | | 77 | 78 | 79 | 80 | 81 | 82 | 83 | 84 | 85 | 86 |

| 87 | 88 | | 89 | 90 | 91 | 92 | 93 | | 94 | 95 | 96 | 97 | 98 | 99 | 100 |

ACROSTIC—PART 1

A) Needs coolant

☐☐☐☐☐☐☐☐☐
60 66 8 25 43 3 97 75 16

B) Good luck doll

☐☐☐☐☐
17 36 79 55 13

C) "Hang ten" surface

☐☐☐☐☐☐☐ ☐
41 63 10 86 61 51 18 5

D) Trudge along

☐☐☐☐
90 33 62 84

E) Showered with gifts

☐☐☐☐☐☐☐☐
82 35 7 74 21 2 65 24

F) North African desert

☐☐☐☐☐☐
92 15 71 58 30 83

G) Liquid preservative

☐☐☐☐☐☐☐☐☐☐☐
14 49 68 89 32 73 20 23 39 85 59 11

H) Lose consciousness

☐☐☐☐☐
52 91 26 19 45

I) Rugrats baby's nickname

☐☐☐☐
37 6 80 64

J) Odor fighter

☐☐☐☐☐☐☐☐☐
69 78 56 4 88 47 67 96 42

K) Part owner

☐☐☐☐☐☐☐☐☐☐☐
38 22 12 57 46 34 54 77 81 28 50

L) Set aside

☐☐☐☐☐☐☐
87 31 9 40 48 27 72

M) It came before the CD

☐☐☐☐☐☐☐☐
53 93 29 1 44 76 70 95

78

ACROSTIC–PART 2
Musical Quote

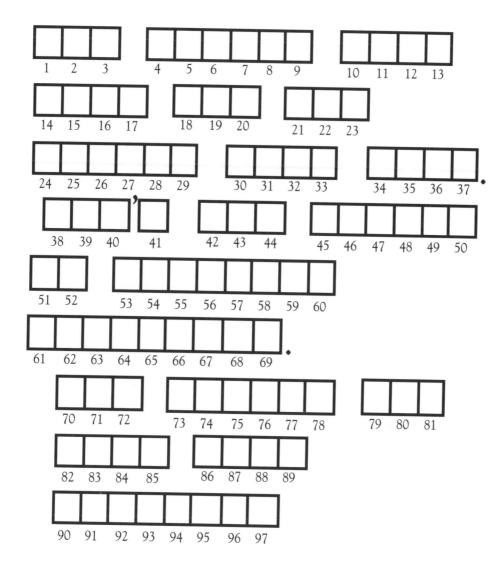

Life's a Beach

sveloh _____

lasetc _____

teolw _____

mulblrea _____

srhtsaif _____

snstue _____

ewasede _____

rdfiualeg _____

einseholr _____

kdroalwba _____

80

Museum Mile

uvlroe   _____

roapd   _____

itmloteporna   _____

zfiiuf   _____

natvcia   _____

amtiehger   _____

ttea   _____

teygt   _____

omudo   _____

igngeemuhg   _____

Connie

_____

_____

Jones

Victor

_____

_____

Blitzer

82

LeTTeR • Shuffle •

Rod	Mellow	Block	Crown	Greek
_____	_____	_____	_____	_____

ANTONYM WORD SEARCH

K	E	E	M	R	P	X	Z	B	L
E	X	R	A	E	L	C	U	W	E
R	I	A	F	I	R	S	T	O	I
Y	M	C	F	A	O	S	C	L	D
T	K	D	I	V	I	D	E	L	J
U	R	W	X	I	V	Y	O	O	A
P	E	E	L	S	A	B	W	F	I
M	R	X	L	A	B	N	O	Z	K
J	O	I	V	A	C	Q	J	E	C

GAEVU

DEECPER

WRYSOD

NICEMOB

IITDM

THECAD

83

it

Takes

Two

Armchair Puzzlers • Word Puzzles

Garry ⌒ _____ ⌒ Mathers

Jennie ⌒ _____ ⌒ Brooks

John ⌒ _____ ⌒ Newton

84

LeTter • Shuffle •

Shire   Moat   Shows   Docks   Beans

_____   _____   _____   _____   _____

ANTONYM WORD SEARCH

A	R	O	P	X	E	D	R	E	W
L	E	S	N	E	W	R	I	O	R
O	T	N	O	R	F	P	U	R	E
H	U	P	Z	L	T	H	D	O	A
S	R	W	K	J	C	E	N	B	K
E	N	Y	C	D	M	G	C	M	J
D	O	U	Y	A	O	X	W	U	Y
A	E	S	T	Y	K	C	T	D	W
C	R	U	Q	I	L	S	I	N	O

OROISEUFC

TDCEIRIN

SRMTA

LAEEV

ITMOS

85

it

Takes

Two

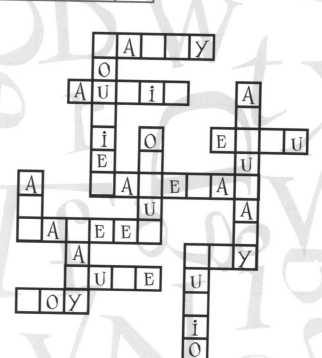

ACROSTIC—PART 1

A) Legal paper

41	13	15	71	7	97	72	66

B) Bug loved by gardeners

30	101	31	105	104	29	95

C) A bad place for a walk

24	84	48	80	1	19	87	

D) Capitol buildings

58	21	4	55	94	43	53	45	26	52	65

E) One traveling for pleasure

34	85	67	33	92	89	44	79	75	77	39

F) Symphonic group

50	96	90	93	57	103	9	82	91

G) Nashville gem

60	16	25	38	11	5	74	81	18	35

H) Small part of something bigger

54	12	98	63	69	37	51	83

I) What Detroit is to the Tigers

22	68	86	40	99	28	3	62

J) Transmission tool

100	76	61	88	46	27	73	14	102

K) Callas specialty

8	36	78	6

L) Pearly whites

2	64	47	59	56

M) Something greatly loathed

42	49	17	10	32	20	70	23

86

ACROSTIC—PART 2
Literary Quote

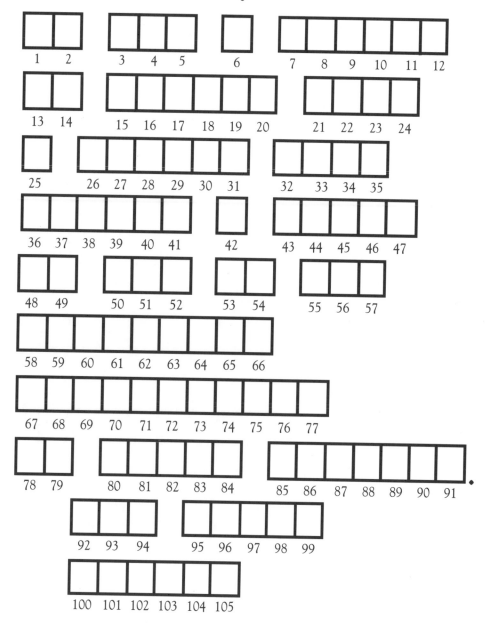

| | |
|1|2|

| | | |
|3|4|5|

| |
|6|

| | | | | | |
|7|8|9|10|11|12|

| | |
|13|14|

| | | | | | |
|15|16|17|18|19|20|

| | | | |
|21|22|23|24|

| |
|25|

| | | | | | |
|26|27|28|29|30|31|

| | | | |
|32|33|34|35|

| | | | | | |
|36|37|38|39|40|41|

| |
|42|

| | | | | |
|43|44|45|46|47|

| | |
|48|49|

| | | |
|50|51|52|

| | |
|53|54|

| | | |
|55|56|57|

| | | | | | | | | |
|58|59|60|61|62|63|64|65|66|

| | | | | | | | | | | |
|67|68|69|70|71|72|73|74|75|76|77|

| | |
|78|79|

| | | | | |
|80|81|82|83|84|

| | | | | | | |
|85|86|87|88|89|90|91|.

| | |
|92|93|94|

| | | | |
|95|96|97|98|99|

| | | | | |
|100|101|102|103|104|105|

87

ACROSTIC—PART 1

A) Ship's cargo log

70	2	50	15	62	37	26	9

B) Golf's Woods

18	40	68	12	21

C) City park denizen

79	30	44	20	71	16

D) Sir

3	67	49	82	19	35

E) Short native African

60	74	51	7	14

F) Light that lingers past sunset

55	52	27	77	29	17	13	53	45

G) Part of a roof

75	36	69	31	6	41	59

H) Painter's need

39	46	56	64	73

I) Decide

25	63	48	22	54	11	4	43	58

J) In an old way

28	24	38	42	78	5	34	57	61

K) At first

47	81	66	1	80	33	65	76	8

L) Acquire

32	23	10	72

88

ACROSTIC—PART 2
Musical Quote

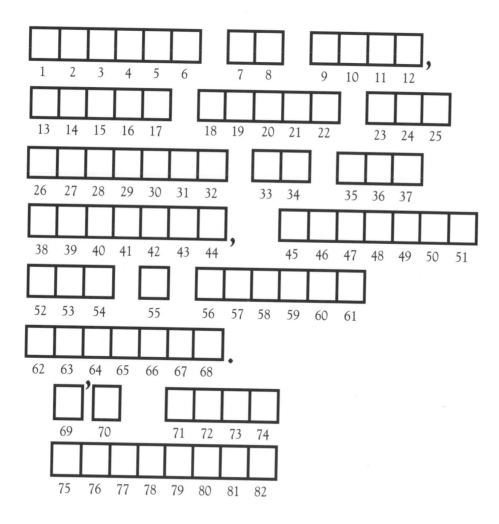

word muddles

It's Not Easy Being Green

90

anebs   _____

asgrs   _____

imktre   _____

gllatioar   _____

gtian   _____

veelas   _____

lrcocbio   _____

mesil   _____

tctleue   _____

oscrmkah   _____

word muddles

It's a Zoo Out There

riglola   _____

inlo   _____

riteg   _____

anheeplt   _____

rabez   _____

kroanoga   _____

reaigff   _____

npgheiu   _____

telaneop   _____

omagilfn   _____

91

BEFORE & AFTER

Johnny ⋯⌢

_____

⋯⌢ Daly

Muhammad ⋯⌢

_____

⋯⌢ MacGraw

Spike ⋯⌢

_____

⋯⌢ Cobb

LeTter •Shuffle•

Booth   Bar   Eke   Nosh   Thin

_____ _____ _____ _____ _____

ANTONYM WORD SEARCH

L	E	W	R	T	K	C	E	E	X
A	L	A	C	I	P	O	R	T	C
C	R	N	R	O	R	I	O	N	I
I	N	Z	A	M	S	A	E	C	B
M	D	G	O	K	F	Z	A	F	R
O	A	I	Y	B	D	R	G	B	E
C	K	D	R	A	I	V	O	L	C
O	M	Y	N	O	T	N	A	O	A
A	S	M	R	A	S	A	R	N	L

ELRSSHMA

ONSNYMY

RAITCC

ESWTE

BSMROE

it
Takes
Two

BEFORE & AFTER

Andrew ⋯⋯ _____ ⋯⋯ Browne

Kobe ⋯⋯ _____ ⋯⋯ Gumbel

Jason ⋯⋯ _____ ⋯⋯ Bell

LeTTer • Shuffle •

Plea   Any   Kite   Poach   Nick

_____ _____ _____ _____ _____

ANTONYM WORD SEARCH

X	C	F	R	L	O	O	R	P	R
O	A	J	Y	H	I	L	E	O	E
L	T	R	A	M	H	V	L	B	H
P	C	O	G	E	A	R	I	S	E
A	T	U	M	Z	O	T	O	C	I
I	S	G	I	A	L	H	U	U	C
Y	F	H	W	C	P	W	I	R	L
E	S	A	E	R	C	E	D	E	E
A	Z	L	N	A	M	R	B	A	Y

ARISENEC

NGOYU

HOSOMT

UMFAOS

LMPETIOI

it

Takes

Two

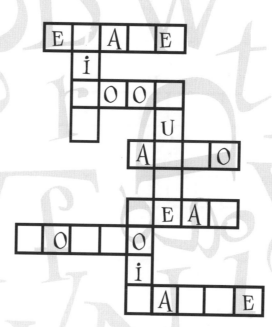

ACROSTIC—PART 1

A) Steer

44	3	74	36	38	68	56	7

B) Like croutons

12	61	17	11	46	39	21

C) Jumping stick

80	9	42	5

D) Basmati or Jasmine

50	84	77	59

E) Frighten

16	71	82	13	1	25	33

F) Tiny bit

58	78	52	41	29	8

G) Dulled

60	51	72	45	87

H) Easygoing

55	48	83	62	67	2	26	70

I) Fibrous veggie

66	14	86	31	18	65

J) Show

76	19	64	43	27	22	34	32	73	49	81

K) Bayed at the moon

57	47	54	4	23	28

L) Body fluid

24	53	63	79	35

M) Instant noodles

10	15	20	85	37

N) Couch

69	75	30	40	6

ACROSTIC—PART 2
Literary Quote

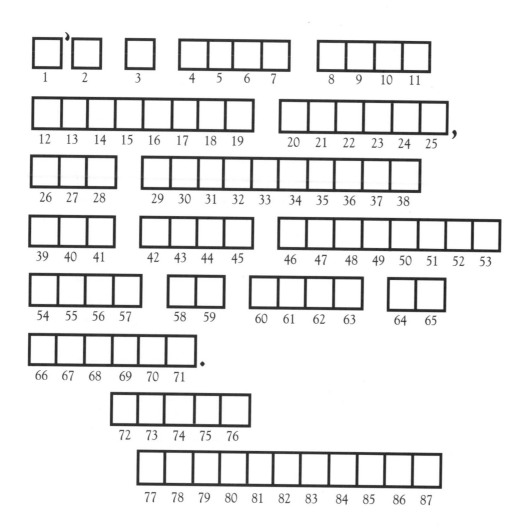

Famous Monkeys

uiuocrs egorge — ——————— — ————————

bnooz — ——————————————

ingk gokn — ——————— — ————————

sbebulb — ——————————————

prega pea — ——————— — ————————

carlem — ——————————————

noihhmchci — ——————————————

ikrfai — ——————————————

pzipy — ——————————————

gikn eluio — ——————— — ————————

ebra — ——————————————

98

Armchair Puzzlers™

Word Searches

Sink Back and Solve Away!™

99

```
R Y R R E H C Q K G B T E Z E
E G B T A O C H C N U R C F L
E R C O C B O M J B T N U M P
F J L O Q A O L R Y T S A J P
F F N R V N L O J Q E E S T A
O U S T R A W B E R R I E S E
T S D E Y N H W G C S K L R N
O E N A I A I P D A C O K A I
W I O E J S P E U R O O N E P
A M M G Z E P C F A T C I B V
L M L F A P Y A T M C E R Y Z
N I A N I U D N O E H Y P M J
U J U H S T N S H L L V S M B
T T W O L L A M H S R A M U P
S D X Q F N C P M L B Q V G P
```

100

SUNDAE SCHOOL

ALMONDS	COOKIES	PECANS
BANANAS	COOL WHIP®	PINEAPPLE
BROWNIE	CRUNCH COAT	SAUCE
BUTTERSCOTCH	GUMMY BEARS	SPRINKLES
CANDY	HOT FUDGE	STRAWBERRIES
CARAMEL	JIMMIES	TOFFEE
CHERRY	MARSHMALLOW	WALNUTS
COCONUT	PEANUTS	WHIPPED CREAM

```
M F S S D S A Q E W C G A A J
W F D Q L Q T O O E H A N G H
Q T N E I T A P M I J X G V P
R C E U P H O R I C I F R E U
O P A L Z R I G L O O M Y A G
Y V A C B R E U U C E C C C I
Y U Y I A A F S Z I R H I Y Z
G H G T R H T M S T E S N E T
C S E N S I T I V E X F A E S
I I L A I V O J R G D Y M U O
M G B M R E P Y H R G L O X P
P G R O U C H Y C E I L M R Q
B U V R S E X Y K N A R C P T
S L L P D S O M B E R W U T E
X S V M J S E X J P W R K X O
```

101

ANGRY

ANXIOUS

BASHFUL

CHEERY

CRANKY

DEPRESSED

ENERGETIC

EUPHORIC

GLOOMY

GROUCHY

HYPER

IMPATIENT

IRATE

IRRITABLE

JEALOUS

JOVIAL

MANIC

ROMANTIC

SENSITIVE

SEXY

SLEEPY

SLUGGISH

SOMBER

TENSE

MOOD
FOR
THOUGHT

```
Y P X R U U C T E E T H I N G
C I O J W A B E Y J T U S Y C
A F W F R S L A S K Q R P R H
C C E S O D B Y B Z E A I E M
K R E L A R D O C Y U S T S C
S A Y R T I M R N C F H U R C
T T C I A T A U E N K O P U A
B G R P N W O R L K E Q O N R
S L E O L G E B C A F T I D R
E R A I L A P A C I F I E R I
I G N N L L S S L O O R D B A
T G V A K K E W H P R U B I G
O I V Z O E H R M T J T Q R E
O Y J U D Z T N Z E A G U C K
B B L B S E L T T A R B Y Z Y
```

102

BABY BOOM

BABY FOOD	BURP	CRIB	PACIFIER
BATHS	CAR SEAT	CRYING	RASH
BLANKET	CARRIAGE	DIAPER	RATTLE
BONNET	CEREAL	DROOL	SPIT UP
BOOTIES	CRADLE	FORMULA	STROLLER
BOTTLE	CRAWLING	NURSERY	TEETHING

```
B T S N Q A L B H W T Q R Z C
N E S E G M A C C H I A T O L
A T I N A R G K O C X C L Y W
U Y E P I U A K A D O U N L S
K X T S E Z L N G H M M U L S
U A T K C S N A D B V U D S E
F A A I A A S E I E X N E H R
J Q L N P M G A N T I L C Z P
M O Y N P E N T T M P E A C H
O O O Y U R I E O I L A F B C
D C S N C I W C H N M D L J N
R Y I O I C H W O V V E F P E
H J J T N A T C L Y H D D Q R
H D R F O N I C C U P P A R F
D O P P I O W O S S E R P S E
```

AMERICANO

AU LAIT

BARISTA

CAPPUCCINO

COLUMBIAN

CON LECHE

CON PANNA

DECAF

DEMITASSE

DOPPIO

ESPRESSO

FRAPPUCCINO®

FRENCH PRESS

GRANDE

GRANITA

MACCHIATO

MOCHA

SKINNY

SOY LATTE

TALL

UNLEADED

VENTI

WHIPLESS

WITH WINGS

CUPPA
JOE
LINGO

```
T T T H O K S T N K O F V Y K
N L E U F R D T H N C U K H J
Y E S L A E B O G F O R C E E
P G R M E N U I O L L O P A D
E R E H P S O M T A U C M X H
D A V H T A C R N N M K I N V
I V I O F C L O T O B E I S H
R I N R F L D P S I T Z N X
Y T U H H U O V R E A S Y P N
L Y J Z C W F T J I N H S Z T
L M V K N W U V F H N U L I E
A I L F U F W J S I E T J T M
S Q B C A B G P O N L T B K B
A R S Z L Y G T B V G L V T J
N B K U M R L O H K R E V O R
```

EARTH BELOW US

ALDRIN	FUEL	LIFTOFF	ROCKET
APOLLO	G FORCE	MARS	ROVER
ASTRONAUT	GLENN	MISSION	SALLY RIDE
ATMOSPHERE	GRAVITY	MOON	SHUTTLE
COLUMBIA	HOUSTON	NASA	TELESCOPE
COUNTDOWN	LAUNCH	ORBIT	UNIVERSE

```
X S M I R N V H H B Y M L A U
D K T D W L C S G S I E Y E M
P V W A F A M W F N S A A E Z
F O H L T R E V E I R T E R S
E P N A W E T S G O O S E O S
T G S D W E W Z D C C Y K J D
V G C E L N T A I G Q P Y P I
O M E M B E R N R I B R I C K
I X F Q N O R U B R A E C B B
V P W Z L C L G E L I C R N Q
Y T E O A E V G T S A O C M V
S V C I C Y N E A O A R R B N
H K R V J I C T G P O D A S L
S Y K H F E P V T X K T E F Y
N R S Q H I M X Z M W G H Z U
```

105

BRICK	GATE BRIDGE	MEMBER	RULE	**GOLD**
COAST	GIRLS	MINES	STATE	**RUSH**
COINS	GLOBES	NUGGET	WARRIORS	
COLORADO	GOOSE	POND	TOOTH	
EGG	HAWN	RECORD	YEARS	
EYE	LOCKS	RETRIEVER		
FINGER	MEDAL			

```
B W N S I N G L E Z S U G U V
H A Y X P N P R G C X V J U S
O L S P F K W R A E P C R B H
J K T E V I R D E N I L B D M
E U R R S J O S R T D L R Z W
T J I F I L I U Q E T S R R O
N P K E O P O L T R H I L Z K
W O E C H U L A P F N C H A Z
K T X T O M L E D I I S T O M
U S T G M P A T P E T E X A N
W T C A E I B S T L D C L W C
J R M M R R Y Z F D A C H D G
V O O E U E L B U O D Y U E L
E H N W N F F A Q W S Z C T R
V S H U T O U T U O G U D U A
```

TAKE ME OUT TO THE BALLGAME

BASES LOADED

BAT

CATCHER

CENTERFIELD

DOUBLE

DUGOUT

FLY BALL

FOUL

GRAND SLAM

HOMEPLATE

HOME RUN

LINE DRIVE

NO HITTER

OUTFIELD

PERFECT GAME

PITCHER

SHORTSTOP

SHUT OUT

SINGLE

STEAL

STRIKE

TRIPLE PLAY

UMPIRE

WALK

```
K O X G X Z X N Q D Q I O R E
P E I T B P M X K L H T U Y E
U K O E X Z V U M U C O N E X
P I N T O W S F N C L Q W T X
K D L F C D L L S I C U Y A U
X N I T G A R B A N Z O A D O
M E O G N I R T S N N A U B I
I Y L L O Y D W R I G H T R P
A F A V A R E E F H N E M N T
H Q Z W O V K Y I S V A L L I
L X N F N S A X J R V D T L R
E E F F O C B A V O F N H R A
F I O V M Y M W P G R E E N A
G L P B Y I Q A W B C M R T L
J J E L L Y G H T W I I H B H
```

AVALON

BAKED

COFFEE

FAVA

FENWAY

GARBANZO

GIFFORD

GORSHIN

GREEN

JELLY

KIDNEY

LANGELLA

LIMA

LLOYD WRIGHT

LYMON

MCCOURT

MUNIZ

OZ

PINTO

REFRIED

SINATRA

STRING

VALLI

WAX

FRANKS AND BEANS

```
W A J D W J O F P F O L O W H
P I N O T N O I R S H G T H J
Z H M A E R C G S I H T F H H
V M O I C O O T O L R E M Z X
Y G F Q T I N P Z B T H R M C
V T N T E N R E B A C S U R B
O G A I S A A E M H R S T S Y
E G R L L X D I M C C I B I V
E D F S L S D U H A N W H F H
Z W B Z R F E X T C R S P S S
B O Z U D N H I T V A S V Y X
Q J K X S R C H R K U D A B P
W W U T I I J W E B V F U L H
K A E Y K O I S I L O D V O A
A R B O W R Z Y R M N U P C G
```

WINE AND CHEESE, PLEASE!

AMERICAN	CHIANTI	GOUDA	PORT
ASIAGO	COLBY	MARSALA	RIESLING
BRIE	COTTAGE	MERLOT	SAKE
CABERNET	CREAM	MUENSTER	SHERRY
CHABLIS	FETA	MUSCAT	SHIRAZ
CHEDDAR	GOAT	PINOT NOIR	SWISS

```
H C D J B W Q O H F G F V B P
G C O N G A S K G A P V E H Z
D T S I W T H N Y O L L T O H
G C T S C U F M H O E I T K U
J E R K W S M Y C C B A N E L
T P O P P I N O T B T U A Y L
I F L H H N M R A O A K M P Y
G K L S U O I R P N O J G O G
C E J B T C R D E Y P B N K U
M Z X I S E E R G L E O I E L
O U O L G H A D A G T K N Y L
W N I O S C I Q B X P S N Y Y
R D R A A A D A B M A L U O P
E X M M O O N W A L K X R H M
E C N A D N E K C I H C O I G
```

109

BUNNY HOP

CABBAGE PATCH

CHICKEN DANCE

CONGA

ELECTRIC SLIDE

HOKEY POKEY

HULLY GULLY

HUSTLE

JERK

LAMBADA

LOCOMOTION

MACARENA

MASHED POTATO

MONKEY

MOONWALK

PONY

POPPIN

ROGER RABBIT

RUNNING MAN

SHIMMY

STROLL

SWIM

TWIST

WATUSI

DANCING DOWN MEMORY LANE

```
D Z Y B H V D X F G X I Z O N
Y L I E W T Q U S Q A T T Y X
O I E W E N W E U B G R G Z Y
R V O E H P I L U T O J M W W
P L F K D R U T O U C A N U T
L K T R L U A O A B Y L N O K
M X A P Y J T N T U E S D A Y
J X E A W H N I H L L F F T O
M B Z E P N O G T A O O O O W
Z R L A A T H H M R C M R D R
S W S D L X R T T F O R M A L
T T E B R N G I E R O F U Y H
E N U T R O F O R G E O L A S
H K V V U Y F O R T Y R A G J
Y O V N C V W O Y S H K D V X
```

110

2 X 4

FORD	FORMULA	TODAY	TOUPEE
FORE	FORT	TOMORROW	TUBA
FOREIGN	FORTIFY	TONIGHT	TUBULAR
FORGE	FORTITUDE	TOOT	TUESDAY
FORK	FORTUNE	TOOTHPASTE	TULIP
FORMAL	FORTY	TOUCAN	TUNA

```
I L Z M J Y X B S U H I Q D P
P I Q A A H G I X N Q M B Q A
K I C N G I B L L O O K U D N
L Z O X N M N H C M P T R H T
O I U O H A T E E H C A M D H
L A G X I L I E C O P B E D E
E R A S N A A R A O B B S S R
M R R Y Y Y R C E W O Y E D C
Z E O D H A L L A B I N M Q T
P G G C U N L X T R I G A Z B
T I N G I O O A D L A S I Q B
J T A C D L I W A W J C S C M
W J J G Y L A B F B R L F S N
D Z A M U P B C L T M G T E Y
I R H H R M R P T M X D E E E
```

111

ANGORA

BALINESE

BOBTAIL

BURMESE

CALICO

CARACAL

CHEETAH

COUGAR

HIMALAYAN

JAGUAR

LEOPARD

LION

LYNX

MAINE COON

MANX

PANTHER

PERSIAN

PUMA

RAGDOLL

SIAMESE

SIBERIAN

TABBY

TIGER

WILDCAT

THE CAT'S OUT OF THE BAG

```
T S F L Q H V G I L O S T I N
P Y M Y F I T S U J A P H R Z
M E M I T S E K A T O U E E G
D W G D C R A Z Y Y C V R D W
A N V R A N W A P N P R E N B
G I I Y O H F P L I W K I E P
Y N S R O O U C G L E O S T O
C O I E E P V O H L O T N E W
J Q O N A G T Y Y A O U E M E
U J N D R O A L K F P R T N R
F O O L D U F N M I I E Y O O
F I F E B A B Y E N N M L O F
P I P S K N I T S E X D M O F
W F O S G N I W E H T N O I F
C R U O Y O D O H W L A M F N
```

LOVE IS IN THE AIR

A TEENAGER IN

ALL OUT OF

BABY

BEST OF MY

BURNING

CHAPEL OF

CRAZY

ENDLESS

GLORY OF

GROOVY KIND OF

IF YOU HAD MY

JUSTIFY MY

LOST IN

ME TENDER

ON THE WINGS OF

POWER OF

PUPPY

SEA OF

STINKS

TAKES TIME

THERE IS

VISION OF

WHEN I FALL IN

WHO DO YOU

112

```
N U Z K V F Y S U P Y T A L P
D U B A R B I E Z B L O K E K
O C L O A T D N J K O A L A Y
E H Y L V P I I M K N I G E G
Y M L E A G T G Z G D A Y D J
X A E U R R K I A O W O Y I G
W A N C I O B R C O P P W N G
M G X A K B O O M E R A N G S
M C C L C O R B R H D L E O E
H N S Y A C A A A P H S N E T
B J R P B T H G L R L L D S W
Q Y A T T O O C I D N A B O E
L V C U U Y I V E G E M I T E
S H X S O P B H H O W I A N Q
S P E P M I R H S U B M Z Z Y
```

113

ABORIGINES

BANDICOOT

BARBIE

BLOKE

BOOMERANG

BUSH

CROCODILE

DINGOES

EUCALYPTUS

G'DAY

KANGAROO

KOALA

MATE

NULLARBOR PLAIN

OPALS

OPERA HOUSE

OUTBACK

PLATYPUS

ROO BAR

SHEILA

SHRIMP

VEGEMITE

WALLABY

WOMBAT

LAND
DOWN
UNDER

```
F S U C C R I O R R L D P F O
Y I P L F Z J V B H M L F V Y
D P W O B N I A R D P H N T K
D F N D R I Z Z L E A K T C H
V O L T W D V Z G L K G J P R
F R Q Y B I S B I U E C U Z E
F E L D D U P G J G X R I X N
C S L O O A H E C E P E B L K
J T C K W T F H R L X D J M S
G O P B N D B L E S O N J E U
S O O I P I I C W Z Y U Q B S
H B N A O G R Y O H O H D Z R
N G C J U R X P H A E T X A T
Y I H M R O T S S I T S J T J
D D O O L F D U S L G N N N Q
```

RIGHT AS RAIN

ACID	DROPS	PUDDLE	THUNDER
BOOTS	FLOOD	PURPLE	UMBRELLA
CLOUD	FOREST	RAINBOW	WIPERS
COAT	HAIL	SHOWER	
DELUGE	LEAK	SLICKER	
DOWNPOUR	LIGHTNING	SPRINKLE	
DRIZZLE	PONCHO	STORM	

```
S X S J R J Y S F E P O R U S
E D M I L H H G E S K G A H E
K X R H V S C O C V D N A W V
T S W A O T R B U T O H Y D O
S H S R C C U O I D Q L L E D
C G E W A R U G R U I E G N S
A N P C T E E S E R I N S O A
R I T O O R P R P F I M I T L
F N N A S U A P R O O M P S N
N N C A H B N E A K C T Q K I
F E A A B P P T E S S U J C L
Y H N I P P O Z P I I B S A R
O V T A O E T T Q F N D U L E
R Z N C D E I R F G E I S B M
C H D A B H A S S L E E V E T
```

115

BLACKSTONE	GLOVES	ROPE	TIGERS
BURTON	HENNING	ROY	TOP HAT
CAPE	HOCUS POCUS	SCARF	WAND
CARDS	HOUDINI	SIEGFRIED	
COPPERFIELD	MERLIN	SLEEVE	
DISAPPEAR	MIRRORS	SMOKE	
DOVES	RABBIT	THE COUNT	

DO YOU BELIEVE IN MAGIC?

```
C R C T H I A U W T Q G V Y Z
H S F S W A M P T H I N G N J
S Y R R M U M M Y D D E R F K
T K A E A N Z R Z R B F E W G
U E N T Y N U H M L I N M E G
E R K S D M V Y Q A G C L L O
C H E N Y U L D N V F M I V D
A S N U T A R E F S O N N Z Z
S D S M I K E W A Z O W S K I
U H T E C A F R E H T A E L L
D A E H N I P A L U C A R D L
E J I T H H F C H C N I R G A
M N N M D A C A T P P C M L E
Q V W E I K O O C G R O V E R
J A S O N A M F L O W S V R D
```

MONSTER MASH

BIGFOOT

COOKIE

DRACULA

ELMO

FRANKENSTEIN

FREDDY

GODZILLA

GREMLINS

GRINCH

GROVER

JASON

LEATHERFACE

LOCH NESS

MEDUSA

MICHAEL MYERS

MIKE WAZOWSKI

MR. HYDE

MUMMY

NOSFERATU

PINHEAD

SHREK

SWAMP THING

THE MUNSTERS

WOLFMAN

116

```
Q L S D I N S P A C E A Y B Q
M U O E B F E R G I E E A A U
K I E R L C C A U S E S D F E
I D S E T R O S G L Y T I F E
N N D S N N A O I N T A R O N
G I C S U E O H P V O O F H L
R M I I Y N L C C E L K G Y A
I R B D N E I I E E R E N M T
C U O O Y A K V Z T C L I M I
H O Y W C D T R E A O N K I F
A Y S N I I A I A R B M I J A
R P R I N C E L T C S E E R H
D L I A G A E R D N A E T R P
K I N G A R T H U R N E C H J
E A M E L I A E A R H A R T F
```

117

AMELIA EARHART	D.B. COOPER	KING RICHARD	QUEEN ELIZABETH
ANDREA GAIL	ELVIS	KONG	QUEEN LATIFAH
AT SEA	FERGIE	LADY DI	REMOTE CONTROL
BOYS	IN SPACE	MISS UNIVERSE	
CAR KEYS	JIMMY HOFFA	PRINCE	TITANIC
CAUSE	KING ARTHUR	PRINCE CHARLES	YOUR MIND
	KING FRIDAY		

LOST AND CROWNED

```
X N L O C N I L Q U S A M M
R I A V R O C D N Q P G O U
V C Q F A I R L A N E D N S
K J A S E I T V Q D E R Z T
A E L L B P D S E L D I A A
O Y P E L E U N T T S B N N
H A R J S I E O L E T R T G
N I D O E A D V C R E E W Q
F S T U D E B A K E R D H I
F O R O C L P R C D C N P T
V O N I M A C L E E A U W Y
V S T I N G R A Y V M H E A
T C H A R G E R H L A T Y D
I C R I M P A L A E R B G B
Z W T E L R R B T B O B K I
```

AMERICAN IDLE

BARRACUDA
BELVEDERE
CADILLAC
CAMARO
CHARGER
CORVAIR

CORVETTE
DESOTO
DEUCE COUPE
EL CAMINO
FAIRLANE
FIREBIRD

IMPALA
JEEP
LE SABRE
LINCOLN
MODEL T
MONZA

MUSTANG
NOVA
SPEEDSTER
STINGRAY
STUDEBAKER
THUNDERBIRD

118

```
V M Q N G O L D T H W A I T F
D Y B Z P R L Q O W C U H X T
M S R Z Y R S P O N G E B O B
M K N V N J E H A S B U Y Y K
W X R U T R S L I U F B H W U
C S M V J E I L I F S A G E T
C U O V D V E L A R W N C O G
W O G I N N D L B A R K E R F
T Q S N T E O E K E E S J R M
H Z A T R D L D D R Z B W O N
J D S O A Z P Y M H E D O Y F
Q Y O N H S B R O W N G Q J K
X L D L W V L N M O J N E P W
M A R L E Y Z C E R F H U S K
I N F D N Q K I R V D K F I C
```

BARKER	DYLAN	NEWHART	SILENT	**WHAT**
BROWN	EUBANKS	ORR	SPONGEBOB	**ABOUT**
BUFFALO	GOLDTHWAIT	RYDELL	THE BUILDER	**BOB?**
COSTAS	HOPE	SAGET	UECKER	
DENVER	MARLEY	SEGER	VILA	
DOLE	MOOG	SIDESHOW	VINTON	

120

LAW AND ORDER

```
C B S W B S P R I X C Y G U S
A E H V Q D L N O B G N S P Z
X R O T C A Z H U B I O D U T
L J R D G O E T C R B L I J K
W R R E S I U R C P L E A U H
X R L A S S J R D R W F R R U
U L N T L T E S T I M O N Y O
I O I Y U G S F E D S U A I J
E N G A D Y R F N N C T P S Y
G T S U B S R U D O T J L I Q
K R J J S O C C B O C E N P S
U J U A T C I D R E V U N X L
J C T K S S E N T I W F V C C
M I S D E M E A N O R G X T E
M I O X W Y S H E Y V U Y A N
```

ALIBI	CONFESS	ILLEGAL	ROBBERY
ARREST	COURT	JUDGE	SENTENCE
ATTORNEY	CRUISER	JURY	STING
BAIL	FELONY	MISDEMEANOR	TESTIMONY
BURGLAR	HANDCUFFS	PLEA	VERDICT
BUST	HEIST	RAID	WITNESS

```
L T S M G N A B B E F N U E S
I C A L O R I Q E T U Q S O P
A S I O I G A B Z G A R E R R
K F D L W P S D T S O O E D I
P L L H B I N R I H E K L S N
E O E E R K I S G O A T B F K
G E O F V U F N L O F M I L L
L X T H Q O I O S I O L I K E
S O E S A R H R G B D A Y D R
N B S F P L E S R Q P E D E X
O D G S I P U E W A S E E S R
R N N Q U W T H G O G G L E S
K A I S G A J U N G L E G Y M
E S W U W S E O H S E S R O H
L Y S F L I P P E R S C T Y K
```

BIG WHEEL®

FLIPPERS

FLOAT

FRISBEE®

GOGGLES

HORSESHOES

HULA HOOP®

JUNGLE GYM

KITES

MASK

NOODLE

PAIL

RADIO FLYER®

SANDBOX

SEESAW

SHOVEL

SLIP 'N SLIDE®

SNORKEL

SPRING HORSE

SPRINKLER

SQUIRT GUN

SUPER SOAKER®

SWING SET

WATER BOMBS

TOYS OF SUMMER

```
D Z Y C I T Y L I G H T S Y G
O G R A L Y E K B E N H U R O
V O O C F T E G H P K B N O X
J L T S D R I B E H T D S T A
O D S L C G I R S H A N E S W
L Y E R I O H C Y S P N T E F
G E V E T U O B A L L A B D O
N L O G I T R E V N R I L I E
O L L B Z V F E A I Q U V S S
K E P B E T I Y S J I U D T U
G R A C N A L B A S A C E S O
N V B A K N O O N H G I H E H
I W I Z A R D O F O Z F C W N
K G M D N U O B L L E P S A L
E T A K E M S S I K C U D R A
```

SILVER SCREEN

A STAR IS BORN

AFRICAN QUEEN

ALL ABOUT EVE

BEN HUR

CASABLANCA

CITIZEN KANE

CITY LIGHTS

GIANT

GIGI

HIGH NOON

HOUSE OF WAX

KEY LARGO

KING KONG

KISS ME KATE

LOVE STORY

OLD YELLER

PSYCHO

SHANE

SPELLBOUND

SUNSET BLVD.

THE BIRDS

VERTIGO

WEST SIDE STORY

WIZARD OF OZ

```
V S H I D H A D C R J X C M A
W H Y M I B M V X I W T J P V
P Z G C A W R U D A Z W W L W
G W G B W T H E I L I I Z D Y
O N I L L A B A K W D B C Q K
G R J H L I S G C S Y Q Z C O
C Q F F C F N S H K R N A B A
G Q K E M I I G U Y E M O H B
R A S Q S G K M B P L D S L G
O B Y S P P Z X O L L O I T P
F U O H H L N D U U I W J R W
J L D O A O A B N B H N K I F
F G U R T V E Y C L C L G P P
W J D T D Y V I E F R O N T E
M O E Y S B M B K R S W E E T
```

BALLIN	CRIB	ILL	SHORTY
BLING BLING	DOPE	JIGGY	SWEET
BOO	DOWN LOW	MACK	TRIP
BOOTY	FLOSSING	PHAT	WASSUP
BOUNCE	FRONT	PLAYER	WHACKED
CHILL	HOMEY	RIDE	YO DUDE

SLANG TIME

```
S K R A Z O G S D O O W D E R
L L E B Y T R E B I L Y D A L
T G N S E D A L G R E V E N E
E E O I T S N E S E H R B E I
U T T E A X D M A O O U U L P
E T S T G G C P L H O S N D P
S Y W I N L A I T A V H K E I
U S O M E Y N R L T E M E E S
O B L E D S Y E A D R O R N S
H U L S L I O S K F D R H E I
E R E O O K N T E E A E I C S
T G Y Y G A L A M O M L L A S
I R K C O R H T U O M Y L P I
H C R A Y A W E T A G S B S M
W D S E A R S T O W E R C T N
```

AMERICA THE BEAUTIFUL

ALAMO

BUNKER HILL

EMPIRE STATE

EVERGLADES

GATEWAY ARCH

GETTYSBURG

GOLDEN GATE

GRAND CANYON

HOOVER DAM

LADY LIBERTY

LIBERTY BELL

MISSISSIPPI

NIAGARA FALLS

OZARKS

PLYMOUTH ROCK

REDWOODS

RUSHMORE

SALT LAKE

SEARS TOWER

SPACE NEEDLE

TAHOE

WHITE HOUSE

YELLOWSTONE

YOSEMITE

```
A Q M U G C V R T G I M Q H M
F B Y E Z W Z T C W J R Q S N
Y P S E S A J C A O E U L F C
E O H V E Q T O D D Y Y R M R
T L U N N D E T D A T S W F E
M P D S T Y O A Y I S N Y F G
F C D D C E L D D U C K Y W S
J R E V I T I D D A J Q B W N
Y Z R L D F O R U B S W P D W
Y P T O D D L E R Y A E T A C
S A A F A D L S C E D L D X N
B L M D D D I S P U D D L E F
K T X D D C M W R P L D U C C
H P E I Y L U E T E E I U M C
P M M E T V E C W L G R G R O
```

125

DOUBLE Ds

ADDRESS	LADDER	PUDDLE	TODDY
CADDY	MIDDLE	RIDDLE	TWIDDLE
CRUDDY	MUDDY	RUDDER	UDDER
CUDDLE	ODDBALL	SADDLE	WADDLE
DADDY	ODDITY	SHUDDER	
FIDDLE	PADDLE	TODDLER	

```
H O T D O G Y F G A K B U S R
G J W M I L K D U D S O Q E A
Q K I L C U H P M B P E T L I
Y A Z J H A O E M M A P A T S
Y Y Z A U P S E Y N C Y K T I
V S L D C N U C B W O K T I N
N W E O K M I K E A N D I K E
J Q R S L M Q O A F S C K S T
U N S R E K A E R B W A J G T
J A R E S E D W S M R Y L N E
U C E P T S R E K C I N S J S
B H B P O W S S N O B N O B Q
E O O O D S E L A M A T T O H
S S O H Y D D A D R A G U S F
C E G W P X N N N F M P S M T
```

MOVIE MUNCHIES

BON BONS®	JUJUBES®	REESES®
CHUCKLES®	JUNIOR MINTS®	SKITTLES®
DOTS®	KIT KAT®	SNICKERS®
GOOBERS®	MIKE AND IKE®	SNO CAPS®
GUMMY BEARS	MILK DUDS®	SODA
HOT DOG	NACHOS	SUGAR DADDY®
HOT TAMALES®	POPCORN	TWIZZLERS®
JAWBREAKERS	RAISINETTES®	WHOPPERS®

```
I D M D E N H H K B M R M Q M
D B J N O O M Y E N O H R K C
S B F I R S T D A N C E U X B
R V N M D I A M O N D R Z V A
X U M A N H S H Y W I Q M H L
K S P R P T F A Q O B D C B B
L N E F L O W E R G I R L R Z
T T O Q D A L I M A U I R P F
E E N I E S Y I M H T U V J K
U X A X I T N S C O R L E D V
Q M M A R I E W A E I G A O U
U Q T W S D L A K A N S W C M
O F S T I I F L E H G S O I E
B C E R E M O N Y D S G E W Q
O R B V Q C U I V J X P K N D
```

127

GOING TO THE CHAPEL

AISLE

ALTAR

BEST MAN

BOUQUET

BRIDESMAID

CAKE

CEREMONY

CHURCH

DIAMOND

ETERNITY

FIRST DANCE

FLOWER GIRL

GOWN

HONEYMOON

IN-LAWS

LACE

LICENSE

MAID OF HONOR

MINISTER

RINGS

TOAST

UNION

VEIL

VOWS

```
U F K R Q E B G Y G I O C C F
P Y C L V V B I S I M K W K E
M R U A O K A U A D J D V J Z
Y R R E B W A R T S F E Y E X
R E T S B O L S T T L D O Z E
F H E A D N G I S P O T S U N
D C R S E F D X P O E N E N X
D N I O O V K A H S T P S T S
L D F X F N T G O O T W P E A
F L X Z X V N P N L E I A E S
D K Z F H I A W D I V S C S R
O K H T D P R D O L R F O K O
A R L I A G D H X L O R I R C
J S R F U F Y P U H C T E K K
N R W B F T H G I L F P Z H S
```

RED-LETTER DAY

APPLE	FOXX	PEPPER
BUTTONS	HEAD	RIDING HOOD
CHERRY	HERRING	ROCKS
CLOWN NOSE	HYDRANT	ROSE
CORVETTE	KETCHUP	SEA
CROSS	LIGHT	SOX
EYE	LIPSTICK	STOP SIGN
FIRE TRUCK	LOBSTER	STRAWBERRY

```
A D N A L E C A R G M D H S J
L M S R X D G S R O J A S T A
L E D E F A P U O C W F U I I
I M R H Y I X R I A O E N U L
C P O T H H E S I T I W G S H
S H C O Q L G I C R A L L P O
I I E M G O O H A O L R A M U
R S R N S L O M I O K T S U S
P B U P E U A D R B C R S J E
K J E P N S U N M B D H E R R
O L U D I T K S L R I G S R O
R T D L S C S A G E V S A L C
F O X N O E D E U S E U L B K
G M U R L E N O L O C E H T I
V S A C C H A R I T Y K V R R
```

129

LONG LIVE
THE KING

BLUE SUEDE

CHARITY

GIRLS

GOSPEL

GRACELAND

GUITAR

HAWAII

HIPS

HOUND DOG

JAILHOUSE ROCK

JUMPSUITS

JUNGLE ROOM

LAS VEGAS

LISA MARIE

MEMPHIS

MOTHER

PRISCILLA

RECORDS

ROCK 'N' ROLL

SUN STUDIO

SUNGLASSES

TCB

THE COLONEL

TUPELO

```
S S K L C K R T S P O O D L E
F N A D K E O N R E I K R O Y
G T H B T C M A L T E S E R D
J T N U R C C H I H U A H U A
C L S K Z E U K D G E T P O C
J S G N O L T O O F R U E M H
V K T E N A D T A E R G H R S
L N T B F G T D Y N T W S A H
M I O F E N W A Y F R A N K U
H L H R L R M S N A H T A N N
K T D W G R N K K A Y E M T D
U O E H A V B A L L P A R K O
G H R C E R E T R I E V E R B
R E S E B O X E R D V N G Y N
C O L L I E K A K M V Z E H G
```

DOG-EAT-DOG

ARMOUR®	DACHSHUND	HOT LINK	POODLE
BALL PARK®	DODGER DOG	KAHN'S®	RED HOT
BEAGLE	FENWAY FRANK	KAYEM®	RETRIEVER
BOXER	FOOT LONG	MALTESE	SABRETT®
CHIHUAHUA	GERMAN SHEPHERD	NATHAN'S®	ST. BERNARD
COLLIE		OSCAR MAYER®	YORKIE
	GREAT DANE		

```
B Q O O L R N Y N D A R K I R
U P L Y D Z S A E Y B O P K M
H H D K A U H A U H I H C C F
U C N C B M A R G A R I T A Z
D S O M B R E R O U X W C R T
R A H T A M S D I M A R Y P D
V S N I A T N U O M C U U O V
Z T N Y P Z O N S C C T A N Z
Y T A D E S E R T A N A S C Q
T R L M C P M V T W L I A H B
E P I N A T A A R I U S C O T
G D A L C L N O U E L Q A P C
Q S A A T P E Q G L C L R R L
H J R T U Y E S C E T Z A U A
Z H U V S T C H I L E C M K U
```

AGUA

AZTECS

CACTUS

CASA

CERVEZA

CHIHUAHUA

CHILE

CINCO DE MAYO

DESERT

JALAPEÑO

MARACAS

MARGARITA

MAYA

MOUNTAINS

PIÑATA

PONCHO

PYRAMIDS

SALSA

SOMBRERO

TACO

TAMALES

TEQUILA

TORTILLA

YUCATAN

SOUTH OF THE BORDER

```
Y D Y L B W B R E K O O N S E
K D M E O M A H J O N G C V T
V A M G N I C A R E S R O H I
C J U D O M C Q K Y A E B X S
N T R I M B A R W T H Y Q U W
M A O R M I R R C K R H D H S
G M U B A L A H D P E O D E L
N S L L G L T L O A M U H H O
B Y E A K I V W R I K N E N T
Z R T C C A E T N G S D I S S
Q E T K A R S O A O P S E U I
A T E J B D E G T W A D F C P
A T V A T S A N A C R E K O P
S O L C O S R I I R C E F J N
J L K K T V U B L T Z N M K L
```

GET LUCKY

BACCARAT

BACKGAMMON

BILLIARDS

BINGO

BLACK JACK

BRIDGE

CANASTA

CASINO

CRAPS

DOMINOES

GREYHOUNDS

HEARTS

HORSE
RACING

KENO

LOTTERY

MAH-JONG

PAI GOW

POKER

POWER BALL

ROULETTE

RUMMY

SCRATCH
TICKETS

SLOTS

SNOOKER

```
J A R Y Z G T L B Q B T U D M
Z K G G I P L N E S A D E M M
J K Z W D E R O L I A T N A S
G B C D S C D N H H S R F P W
B U Z O J E C H W A R U C O I
G S O A X I E T E B F L R K M
O J O U E P I R T S N I P E R
V G T C P E B T S A I L O R W
K N N W A E C N I U C B W B B
D I Z I L R B L K N C D Z Q P
W G P B H H A S O S H K Q A C
C G U O F T W W P W H Z E X Z
D O B D I N A M R A N H N R P
D J K Y H E U B E L C F N I T
N F Y F I J F Q E G V E O A Q
```

SUIT YOURSELF

133

ARMANI	DOUBLE-BREASTED	PINSTRIPE	SWIM
BATHING	ITALIAN	POKER	TAILORED
BODY	JOGGING	SAILOR	THREE-PIECE
CAT	JUMP	SANTA	TUXEDO
CHEAP	LAW	SEERSUCKER	WET
CLOWN	LEISURE	SPACE	ZOOT

```
C R Y S F L O G N I T A K S R
W R E S T L I N G R Q V O Q T
Z G I R E C C O S N W U T U B
E H O C K E Y P R D I S T A V
S X B V K J B G A S V H H S Z
W N R A N E T N C E O B S H F
S T N B S Z T I Q S L S B I F
W F U O A K T P U S L O A O F
I P X X J S E C E O E F O L V
M R K I A A E T T R Y T R O C
M L G N F B V B B C B B K P Z
I L M G Z A M E A A A A C T D
N Y R E H C R A L L L L A N F
G D B I G S U L L I L L R E A
P G O P V Q Z S I N N E T F W
```

WHAT A GOOD SPORT!

ARCHERY	FOOTBALL	PING PONG	SQUASH
BASEBALL	GOLF	POLO	SWIMMING
BASKETBALL	GYMNASTICS	RACQUETBALL	TENNIS
BOXING	HOCKEY	SKATING	TRACK
CRICKET	JAVELIN	SOCCER	VOLLEYBALL
FISHING	LACROSSE	SOFTBALL	WRESTLING

134

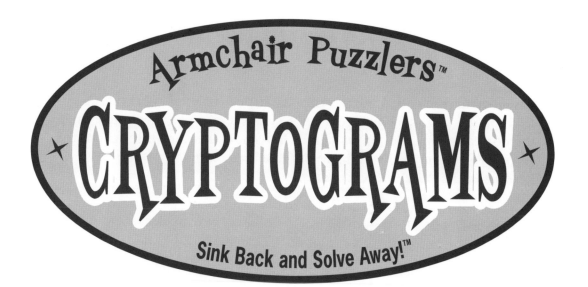

Armchair Puzzlers™

CRYPTOGRAMS

Sink Back and Solve Away!™

135

Instructions

Cryptograms are coded puzzles that are solved by letter substitution. Each puzzle has its own secret code to crack. Once you determine what the correct substitution is for a given letter, it is the same throughout the puzzle. For example, if you figure out that X=A, then every time "X" appears in the puzzle, it will equal "A."

Groups

A group of 10 related items is listed in code under a subject title (i.e., "Beatles Songs"). Use the subject as a starting point to help you crack the code.

Quotes

The quotes are from movies, TV shows, books, celebrities, historical figures and song lyrics, and are in some way linked to the Groups above them.

Remember, each page consists of two separate puzzles, each with its own secret code! There are also **Hints** on page 178 if you need them.

Beatles Songs

Jfao Uo Ef

Yfuoxnzcp

Cf Komjt

Nojxok Ysojxok

Noko Dfuoy xno Ybc

Jox Zx Ho

Tojjfv Ybhuwkzco

Xvzyx wce Ynfbx

Dfuo Xfpoxnok

Ozpnx Ewty a Voos

.... • ....

Quote

"M blyno Eykj Sojjyj, 'M wyj'n

dosmopo mj nko Doxnsoc, M elcn

dosmopo mj fo.' Hyyw rymjn

nkouo. Xqnou xss, ko ixc

Nko Ixsulc."

Qouumc Dlossou'c Wxg Yqq

Italian Dishes

Qruhwiccj

Gjyiqcmayi

Mjhucayj

Hyavvwj

Vuyyiooayj

Ruyjyj

Mudjaoj

Ojyhejyj

Ouquhyu

Camcioojyj

Quote

"Hjgrodllc wgb td dgldb
ymhl hawwdhhpaqqv cp vma
cbogqd cl qcid g zgwaay
wqdgbdf."

—Hmjocg Qmfdb

U.S. State Capitals

Blfpro Btnz, Ohglxl

Nlsslalpphh, Ysrftxl

Ahshol, Kronlol

Dlnro Frcvh, Srctptlol

Kronqhsthf, Ghfkron

Plbflkhonr, Blstyrfotl

Arorscsc, Aliltt

Dtpklfw, Orfna Xlwrnl

Toxtlolqrstp, Toxtlol

Ehyyhfpro Btnz, Ktpprcft

Quote

"Szgkfy jwpk qo Spkvo Evznf,

cpqkqon jve p kepqo,

poy Q cpg jffwqon ofpewi pg jpyfy pg bi afpog.

Svssi klzbsfy p yqfgfw yvco

azgk sfjvef qk epqofy,

klpk evyf zg pww klf cpi kv Ofc Vewfpog."

"Bf poy Svssi BhNff"

—Apoqg Avdwqo

'90s Best Picture Oscars®

Rwgqli zumd Zphbli

Vpeelim Tnas

Waleuqwg Jlwnmk

Ngvpetublg

Idwolislwel ug Hpbl

Mumwguq

Mdl Iuhlgql pv mdl Hwaji

Mdl Lgthuid Swmulgm

Jewbldlwem

Iqdugrhle'i Huim

Quote

"Cfrdr'z s ntaardrpbr hrckrrp qz.

Xmq cftpv cfr ormoer ma cftz espn rltzc

cm odmutnr xmq ktcf omztctmp. T cftpv xmqd

omztctmp rltzcz cm odmutnr cfmzr ormoer

ktcf adrrnmi. Spn T jm cm isvr zqdr

cfsc cfrx fsur tc."

Hdsurfrsdc

Famous "Bills"

Esmmh olw Isu

Esmm Fjowv

Esmm Ymsaoza

Esmm Yzveh

Esmmh Eze Olzxaoza

Esmmh Yxhvojm

Esmmh Bzwm

Esmm Ncxxjh

Esmmsw Lzmsujh

Esmm Njlwx

Quote

"Nfgy O hoxmw mwuxwga orbxkcomoyp

uw Mgikya Iowq, O num mk sua O nuzdga

khh uya aoay'w ikrg suid hkx, zodg,

wnk qguxm. Wfgy O elmw zocga u zowwzg

uya iurg suid nowf u zkw rkxg bgxmky

wk kbgxuwg nowf."

—Sozz Rlxxuq

Constellations

Vlffjiksjl	Lrobitsol
Ybfl Tlqib	Ibjir
Kshlfyf	Ksbfsyf
Ybfl Tjrib	Hstjrj
Msbvywsf	Flhjaalbjyf

Quote

"Wbzcdszcw sd obgrj wdbu vhsisit rbit

cibgtf abv dfc wdhvw db ebzc bgd,

hij dfci sd ohw isec. Sd ohw rsyc ngwd qcabvc

dfc wgi tbcw db qcj jboi bi dfc qhmbg.

Dfcvc ohw hrohmw h zsrrsbi wuhvyrcw

bi dfc ohdcv."

Abvvcwd Tgzu

Cartoon Characters

Vsge Jmibjno

Lqrzpyvyggh Lnqof

Vqcj Vqooh

Vyswmj sof Vqeelysf

Vqppumozpy A. Innjy

Hncm Vysg

Kgyf Kpmoejenoy

Imrzyh Inqjy

Ypiyg Kqff

Vyeeh Vnnb

Quote

Xspah: "Gwzzoqbazr, qk mlhm frxr kflk ysx
hsw ks qbfrxqk kfr ysxkwbr, hsw flir ks
mjrbe kfr orrarbe qb Lgsvqblgzr Vlbsx."

Gwzzoqbazr: "Kflk'm bs jxsgzrv. Q'ir
grrb zqiqbd qb lb lgsvqblgzr vlbbrx
lzz vh zqyr."

Kfr Gwzzoqbazr Mfso

Asian Foods

Xvmgmcpwhng   Pave Lhcd

Xui Mauc   Ly Gay Xudpuwhg

Gygac   Gxncdo Nvqqg

Evd Mvdg   Gehhm udi Gvyn Gvyx

Mhnckuwc   Mhlxynu

Quote

"Crlch pmlrlhd lr c yct oa yaj obfamib

klxd. Lx tam pmfft oaa wcht xcsafr,

tamf xfldhnr ylkk qd oaxm."

—Rblfkdt Xahi-Oaffdr

'70s Best Picture Oscars®

Foyyua

Ymv Eytah

Oaatv Monn

Ymv Pvvz Mlayvz

Uav Xnvg Ukvz ymv Qlqcuu'e Avey

Ymv Hupxoymvz

Ymv Hupxoymvz Fozy TT

Zuqcs

Czoivz ke. Czoivz

Ymv Xzvaqm Quaavqytua

.... ❖ ....

Quote

"M zxdmfhvaujhs, H fjhaq, hu dhqx m ujmzq.

Nve qavb? Hf jmu fv yvaufmafdn lvox pvzbmzr

vz hf rhxu. Mar H fjhaq bjmf bx'ox ivf va vez

jmaru hu m rxmr ujmzq."

Maahx Jmdd

Zafidjs jc dax Jzxwf *Nfde*

Gxe Skexwfmgxe *Naknftj*

Dax Zwjyqnxwe *Tqpe fiy Yjgge*

Dax Lkit fiy K *Dax Gkji Lkit*

Bxed Ekyx Edjwp *Xrkdf*

Quote

"R xros otuiz'q xurku vuy uiltyq,

wq wiz'q erwy rzo wq'i ztq zwlu.

R xros otuiz'q mrzouy rxx tkuy qvu ytta

rzo jxtm tz itau tqvuy hbs'i owlu."

"Xblf Ju r Xros"

Hbsi rzo Otxxi

Oprah's Book Club Picks

Mct Okawkhpkkg Zaznt

Gdlrcmtf kv Vkfmlht

Cklwt kv Wdhg dhg Vkr

Mct Oankm'w Pavt

Pcamt Kntdhgtf

Wkhrw ah Kfgahdfu Mast

Mct Ctdfm kv a Pksdh

Rdo Efttq

Wct'w Ekst Lhgkht

Kht Clhgftg Utdfw kv Wknamlgt

Quote

"Mqf hwm oyrtp w mqyh wsyxu
Gerftom' grtwk nfwe...wto R, xtgyeuxtwufkn,
wv ytf yg uqymf skruqfertp roryum hqy berfo yt
Ydewq. R byxkot'u muyd vnmfkg."

— Ifttrgfe Wtrmuyt

James Bond Movies

E Zniu pq e Gnxx

Wsqa Sljjne unpc Xqzi

Yni Edqpcis Yeo

Yneaqdyj esi Wqsizis

Xnzi edy Xip Yni

Ys. Dq

Mqxywndmis

Qfpqkljjo

Pci Xnzndm Yeoxnmcpj

Pci Jko Ucq Xqziy Ai

Quote

"M qnui nyzntg qnsiv sqns vnok

Enoig Chkv. M'v ympi sh pmyy qmo."

— Gink Fhkkibt

Earth's Islands

Nlccsbfl	Zyabrs Bkfs
Sljy	Nlulpliflb
Dsbmas	Pbaamclmu
Pbalr Dbkrlkm	Vlnlkfl
Lmrkpyl	Dabnyul

Quote

"Askb wez lhg kezpz wez buvewx hpz vhg,

hba wez xyb xeubzx ahufg sb wez qsybwhub wsi,

U wssj h wpui sb h xhufubv xeui

hba kezb U pzhdeza Rhqhudh U qhaz h xwsi."

"Rhqhudh Ohpzkzff"

—Ehppg Lzfhosbwz

Board Games

Nfdsg Bfds

Wpdphpbg

Kmtdkg Uotzkrpdz

Jfbstasfzy

Kyt Xfwt pq Brqt

Nbot

Karirfb Hoazork

Znafjjbt

Nyoktz fds Bfsstaz

Hrnkrpdfag

Quote

"J eap qrf reqfs bpm sjnf qrfxf.

Ke dew ubp gxfqqd zwur kbd qrbq zd

sjlf jk sjyf Zepegesd."

Qae Affyk Peqjuf

Types of Wine

Tlxspkx

Mlqffo

Clxkq Vxpnspjqz

Wqfzhk

Tlsfjhppso

Yxphk Phxf

Tlsazxm

Tsaqfpqk Mseuxbphp

Yhfk

Fhmq

Quote

"R'j zgqb xvunp ezge vrez erlb,

eezufszex ut huf vufoj obgqb lh zbgj.

R vgx vnups gpj R trpj,

dfxe upb ezrps lgwbx lb tunsbe."

"Nbj, Nbj Vrpb"

— Pbro Jrglupj

Al Pacino Movies

Zubtd bn l Ihslt

Zulvnlub

Pebtplvvj Pebt Vhzz

Zbvmouh

Nvltqob ltc Ahyttj

Ulveodh'z Ilj

Dyb Phcnldybv

Lfdyhv! Lfdyhv!

Zbl hn Ehwb

Ltj Powbt Zftclj

Quote

"Ajgvx, kxr'jg dk xhvgj zjxmbgj

cov P hxwg kxr, zrm vxo'm gwgj mcqg

epvge ypmb cokxog clcpoem

mbg acdphk clcpo. Gwgj."

Mbg Lxvacmbgj

Musicians Known By One Name

Hrofkkr	Thbkth
Ivtn	Gxbkl
Utiz	Uyfnz
Tkpr	Ytetw
Ufkf	Grot

- ❖ -

Quote

"Ua u jyer aquj,

X cuzn qiy xoaqxoeqa:

X iuoq qy cuzn wbo uok X

iuoq qy ecuopn qcn iyjtk.

X cuzn u ecuoen qy ky hyqc."

— Hyoy

Major League Baseball
Hometowns

Leyytwfsvc   Crftyrx   Tbx Jsbxoetor

Xgh Ursp Oeyu   Agysrey   Bymbxyb

Ty. Mrfet   Tgbyymg   Oexoexxbye

                    Wrtyrx

Quote

"Eqjm B exi x icxss dhv bm Lxmixi, x rwbjmg hr cbmj xmg B ejma

rbiqbmn. B ahsg qbc B exmajg ah dj x wjxs Cxfhw

Sjxnyj Dxijdxss tsxvjw, x njmybmj twhrjiibhmxs sblj Qhmyi Exnmjw.

Cv rwbjmg ixbg aqxa qj'g sblj ah dj Twjibgjma hr aqj Ymbajg Iaxaji.

Mjbaqjw hr yi nha hyw ebiq."

— Gebnqa G. Jbijmqhejw

'60s Best Picture Ocsars®

Jmogqubq tv Mgmilm

Oqpe Plfq Petgn

Sn Vmlg Jmfn

M Smu vtg Mjj Pqmptup

Slfulyze Btoitn

Ezq Mxmgesque

Ets Wtuqp

Ezq Ptauf tv Saplb

Tjlkqg!

Lu ezq Zqme tv ezq Ulyze

Quote

"Mu iar fmte umtjk dxi wdx nvr tdi n bnjw,

wdx ymbb lr infrt id iar Idyrv du Bdtjdt

yarvr wdxv arnj ymbb lr pxi duu nk

n ynvtmte id diarv zvrkxgzixdxk

ubdyrv emvbk!"

Gw Unmv Bnjw

Email Providers

zzz.byclsweqd.qbl

zzz.yiw.aio

zzz.qblvaykb.aio

zzz.ubcetiq.aio

zzz.rxqi.aio

zzz.nysii.aio

zzz.ovq.aio

zzz.siloyew.aio

zzz.fzbvl.aio

zzz.aiokxvbcub.aio

Quote

"Vy fwx'a aone ohwia oxzakdxs

cymbwxon. Vy rofy o miny ohwia akoa.

D fwx'a exwv kdb xory, vkoa ky fwyb

wm yloganz vkymy ky ndqyb, bw da

vdnn hy myonnz yobz aw bawc

byydxs kdr, hygoiby D'r xwa."

Zwi'qy Swa Rodn

Ice Cream Flavors

Rlye Hqlm

Hqdhdfcev

Kdhub Kdcs

Hddulvp cys Hkvcr

Wxeevk Mvhcy

Nkvyhq Jcylffc

Hdhdyxe

Pekcgwvkkb

Yvdmdflecy

Hdnnvv

Quote

"E'g wepa sna yea naksag kmg E gxm's
vkms sna eia izakq xm sxy, E vkms es
xm sna lega. Kmg E'g wepa lszkvjazzh
emlsakg xd bkmewwk ed hxo nkba es.
Ed mxs, snam mx eia izakq, rols vneyyag
izakq, jos xmwh ed es'l zakw. Ed es'l xos xd
sna ikm, snam mxsnemt."

Vnam Nkzzh Qas Lkwwh...

Armchair Puzzlers • Cryptograms

The Works of Shakespeare

G Khzdckkab Lhtfq'd Zbagk

Kgrmaqf

Qfa Rukazn uj Abbubd

Qfa Qgkhlt uj qfa Dfbax

Qfa Kabbn Xhwad uj Xhlzdub

Bukau glz Scvhaq

Uqfavvu

Kcrf Gzu gmucq Luqfhlt

Fgkvaq

Qfa Qxu Talqvakal uj Wabulg

Quote

"Umh shqpsrpcfh umojb pcatu Xmprhxihpsh

ox umpu mh shpffw ox lhsw baag,

oj xiouh ae pff umh ihaifh zma

xpw mh ox lhsw baag."

— Sachsu Bsplhx

Famous "Georges"

Qudequ Jontbur

Qudequ Tbeeokdi

Qudequ P. Vfkt

Qudequ Gdeujbi

Nfeodfk Qudequ

Qudequ Nrddiuw

Vdw Qudequ

Qudequ J. Ndtbi

Qudequ Rfnbk

Quiuebr Qudequ K. Sbccdi

Quote

"Sfl mefv, rc'k p kypha Iaftia'k dptaeck

qrqe'c iac qrjftxaq cyrtcs saptk pif.

Ya xfloq ypja zaae efthpo."

Karenaoq

Scary Movies

Jfbaloxig uj Gmo Tliggl	*Tzigxo*
Axmmuqggj	*Lag Tfdla Tgjtg*
Rifbal Jfbal	*Lag Gduizftl*
Lag Lgdxt Zaxfjtxq Oxttxzig	*Stvzau*
Jfbal ur lag Mfpfjb Ygxy	*Lag Ohoov*

Quote

"E'c luekl nu xdabj juq iux
fdnxbjekl cd; E'c luekl nu lerd ngbn
fxbek ui juqxt b kdy gucd ek ngd
tvqmm ui ngd Ixbkvdktndek cuktndx."

Guqtd ui Ixbkvdktndek

Cosmetics
Manufacturers

Mozx

V'Zdamv

Cmdu Hmu

Wvyxynla

Iakrzdm

Wzoad Bydv

Cmusavvyxa

Vmxwzca

Wrmxav

Ldsmx Eawmu

Quote

"Ehhs ewxc, fz cho xhg'i zfgx

w uwaafi dfij efktifys wbotfgv,

ijqg cho wgx F jwrq ghijfg' ih twc

ih qwyj hijqu!"

— Aovt Aoggc

Children's Fairy Tales

Qnll wh Siirl

Rfnusjawhd

Riu Rfnus

Rfj Qxwhgjll dhk rfj Qjd

Fdhlja dhk Pxjrja

Sjdnrz dhk rfj Sjdlr

Rfj Yxip Qxwhgj

Xnuqjalrwarlewh

Awrraj Xjk Xwkwhp Fiik

Cdge dhk rfj Sjdhlrdae

Quote

"Pidz d xwo ijdtz W idkj, zij xjzzjt zn unkj enl pwzi.

Uwzzuj Tjc Twcwvo Innc, jkjv xdc pnukjy adv xj onnc.

W'uu zte zn qjjs ydzwyrwjc, blyz zn pduq xe enlt ywcj.

Gdexj enl'uu yjj ziwvoy ge pde, xjrntj pj ojz

zn Otdvcgd'y sudaj."

"Uwzzuj Tjc Twcwvo Innc"

—Ydg zij Yidg dvc zij Sidtdniy

Jewelry Gems

Hnvp

Vlgbqudb

Msvlhtm

Lvpvfqsbg

Vljgy

Avytgb

Ywju

Jpwg Bhnve

Ovmg

Htui

Quote

"Rciql bhgg nycq xkiqh jyjhuvx. Vahn

iqh gezh cufcv leijyulx. Lexfiql vahj

iul vaheq migch begg uhmhq dh zuybu.

Ejkqymh vahj iul vahn begg

dhfyjh vah dqeravhxv rhjx eu i cxhtcg geth."

— Qigka Bigly Hjhqxyu

Diet Fads

Ldowa Yukea Hxuw

Lekclhkru Hxuw

Ukw Cxqaw zdc fdoc Wfgu

Hc. Kwixbl' Hxuw

Qckguzcoxw Hxuw

Yusucrf Axrrl Hxuw

Tklwucxbq wau Mdbu

Gcxwxixb Hxuw

Ekyykqu Ldog Hxuw

Bukbhuc-Waxb: Ukw Rxiu k Eksutkb

Quote

"Ib uqvg cqmm nvlbtv zmm gwv ezg enbl xbhn kbux kvfzhjv gwv knzqi qj vigqnvmx ezg. Cqgwbhg z knzqi, xbh lqrwg mbbs rbbu, khg zmm xbh fbhmu ub qj nhi ebn dhkmqf beeqfv."

— Rvbnrv Kvniznu Jwzc

Elvis Presley Songs

Oula Va Sadkac

Gca Jum Oudafuva Sudtwys?

Yumdk Kuw

Fmfrtitumf Vtdkf

G Otssoa Oaff Iudlacfgstud

Yagcsncagq Yusao

Kud's Na Icmao

Pgtoyumfa Cuiq

Nmcdtdw Oula

Goo Fyuuq Mr

·· ⋆ ··

Quote

"Il [Lcpjh] kvh vh ojt vh bil kircl yrxubsd jbhlcz, vh ojt
vh bil kircl qslvf. Il nxhb lforqjlq bil lhhluyl rz jb vuq il kvh ju
frsbvc yrfovb kjbi bil bijut. Urbijut kjcc lpls bvwl bil gcvyl
rz bivb txd."

— Osxyl Hgsjuthbllu

'80s Best Picture Oscars®

Bwsdklwt Uqbuaq

Hlksyd

Bvf bc Lcwdzl

Ualfbbk

Wldk Xlk

Zylwdbfp bc Cdwq

Fqwxp bc Qksqlwxqkf

Lxlsqvp

Fyq Alpf Qxuqwbw

Swdmdkh Xdpp Sldpt

Quote

"Rgcr tck lxngr rgyly xu tf zlbrgyl cks

xo gy sbyuk'r nyr rb ecrdg *Qybqjy'u Dbilr* xk czbir rgxlrf

uydbksu, gy'u nbkkc rglbe c oxr lxngr gyly bk fbil qbldg.

Kbe fbi dck gyjq ty bl fbi dck urcks rgyly cks

ecrdg xr gcqqyk."

Lcxk Tck

Tropical Fruit

Vtstst   Xtxtut

Tdfktaf   Ntsbf

Xqshtxxwh   Botdt

Xtzzqfs Mpoqj   Xfnhbptstjh

Rqiq   Xtixti

Quote

"Hk hwrmsx fnafkj djsp rw jfk,

'Rms wnpsx kwd vsr, rms isrrsx

kwd vsr, dgnsjj kwd'xs f ifgfgf.'"

Vwnpsg Vzxnj

167

Armchair Puzzlers • Cryptograms

Sesame Street® Characters

Rbwanl ldb Swfj   Jwfibw

Znj Znwc   Fhypw ldb Jwfqyd

Bkaf   Zbwl

Gkpyncf Skpanujf   Bwunb

Yffrnb Afuhlbw   Yfqul ifu Yfqul

Quote

"G zniwhc vdjdk xdds r hdudvc.

Gs'z rharmz cgzrqqigvsgvu, hgfd snd sgxd

G xds Lgu Lgkc rs snd God Orqrcdz:

nd'z vis zi lgu."

Aghh & Ukrod

U.S. Presidents

Bnhbibd Gepwcgp

Thcyzh Wgzyzgbpj

Tzhbgj Lchj

Uizcjchz Hcckzyzgu

Ocip L. Xzppzjs

Tzchtz Mbkieptucp

Oedds Wbhuzh

Abwibhs Ubsgch

Wizkuzh B. Bhuivh

Vgskkzk K. Thbpu

Quote

"Epi wxle bxaiychr wnt mt epi

Htmeiv Leneil ml Byilmvite Tmzxt.

Oxh'ji pinyv xc pmw?"

Nrr epi Byilmvite'l Wit

Julia Roberts Movies

Fvddm Bikjzmyif

Bg Qdfv Nhydjl'f Sdllyjk

Hcjisig Qhyld

Uzza

Fmddryjk syvu vud Djdbg

Vud Rdmywij Qhydn

Rhdvvg Szbij

Nmivmyjdhf

Dhyj Qhzwazoywu

Bgfvyw Ryeei

Quote

"Bn'c vgttd lqjt ojaomj csd,

'B eat'n nqbtz Wgmbs mbzjc pj.'

Qatjd, bv B eat'n mbzj dag,

dag'kj iabti na ztal shagn bn."

— Wgmbs Kahjknc

Chocolate Cravings

Lcggstk	Ribhtsm
Sjm Jimqo	Jqdm
Jqtgv Rqi	Picxxfm
Obcyym	Nbp Jbjbq
Xbtgcm	Nbp Xcgkm

Quote

"Yfi awziplvplyc vs kfvkvnbyi,

dvyf svp fibnyf bjr jvwplafoijy,

tlnn avvj hlxi ly yfi aboi zpisipijki

vxip yib bjr kvssii lj Boiplkb

tflkf ly fba lj Azblj."

— Yfvoba Qissipavj

Earth's Volcanoes

Rg. Puhurlcklon

Rg. Dgcl

Sdjuh'e Gnmdo

Rg. Vnns

Tlolybguc

Rg. Qbku

Rg. Jdebjube

Rg. Eg. Vdhdce

Rg. Hleedc

Polplgnl

Quote

"L yrdu puzz oyrf zlm asfoyz

os pldu. Oyu Irksflz gupludu oyuq fuun

r yjarf zrbvlclbu sv oyulv lzprfn lz tslft

os zlfh lfos oyu sburf. Oyuq yrdu r alfuvrp

oyro qsjv croyuv irfoz zs yu ylvun au

os purk lfos oyulv dspbrfs."

Xsu Duvzjz oyu Dspbrfs

Rolling Stones Songs

Nypz Fykqolz

Qflnf Ak Yh

Rdaak Qvkwfkn

Pklqf bm Pynoki

Lirdk

Vbigz Fbig Xbaki

(D Jli'f Rkf Ib) Qlfdqmljfdbi

Pnbxi Qyrln

Yiokn Az Fvyap

Qzahlfvz mbn fvk Okudw

Quote

"La icd pslhv pstp Kluv Etbbwm

qloo rploo gw xclhb psw qscow

mcuv rptm pslhb tp tbw alapi,

qwoo, pswh, icd tmw rcmwoi,

rcmwoi klrptvwh."

Tokcrp Atkcdr

Children's Authors

Peanmog Xguzew

Deane Muceddx Tmdzgn

Ksg Hnvksgnx Cnmpp

Y. W. Nvtdmuc

Zn. Xgaxx

Pezgdgmug D'gucdg

Nvedz Zesd

Dgpvuj Xumowgk

Lneuw D. Heap

Nmosenz Xoennj

Quote

"Kasj wyg tsaze'q eggngqw sdgfr,

Kasj tfp estr ugzst,

Kasj estr cr wyg jle tygag wyg eggn-ecmgaq bs,

Kasj estr cr wyg jcag fre wyg jldx fre wyg jlax,

C jcbyw dfwdy qsjg kcqy tys fag fzz bscrb,

'BZLAX!'"

JdGzzcbsw'q Nssz

— Ea. Qglqq

Audrey Hepburn Movies

Rxggp Rwuc

Fwetogw

Wqswpf

Etcwirwfj wj Jorrwgp'f

Qznc og jmc Wrjctgzzg

Tzeog wgl Vwtowg

Tzvwg Mzqolwp

Vp Rwot Qwlp

Swt wgl Acwuc

Swoj xgjoq Lwti

Quote

"Z rfd fdtmb ny fgn rkmc Z gyvubc'n fgn.

Z rfd fdtmb ny dzch *Ivcce Ifgm* rkmc

Z gyvubc'n dzch, fcb ny bfcgm rznk

Ijmb Fdnfzjm rkmc Z gyvubc'n bfcgm

— fcb ny by fuu tzcbd yi nkzchd Z rfdc'n

wjmwfjmb iyj. Nkmc Z njzmb uztm pfb

ny gywm rznk zn."

— Fvbjme Kmwqvjc

Countries & Their Capitals

Vihwoh, Bgiop

Dwlbbjtb, Djtxolv

Piowado, Rjpfi

Hldtop, Owjtiph

Dlhigjbs, Elpxiwf

Giwob, Zwipmj

Djocopx, Meopi

Vipoti, Geotoggopjb

Pjn Hjteo, Ophoi

Ejtbopro, Zoptiph

Quote

"Nm pze fgi jektp irzeqa bz afdi

jndiy nr Ufgnc fc f pzerq wfr,

bair haigidig pze qz mzg bai gicb

zm pzeg jnmi nb cbfpc hnba pze,

mzg Ufgnc nc f wzdifsji mifcb."

— Igricb Aiwnrqhfp

British Landmarks

Fbt Faq

Iyjeav Lbdal

Jpfali Yjpp

Vi. Njkp'v Ujiyaxljp

Imsal mh Pmqxmq

Vimqayaqta

Saviebqvial Jffaw

Kqbdalvbiw mh Mzhmlx

Iljhjptjl Vokjla

Fkurbqtyje Njpjua

Quote

"Sqnfzpzkh msf lpz Dhkjnsl, zbh xqnlenxkh py

Daiibnfc nf lpz 'huhqw csl ypq bncfhky', sli zbh Kplipl Alihqjqpali

nf lpz s xpknznesk cpuhchlz."

— S Ynfb Eskkhi Mslis

Cryptograms Hints

Groups

PAGE/HINT	PAGE/HINT	PAGE/HINT	PAGE/HINT	PAGE/HINT	PAGE/HINT
137 E=D	138 H=G	139 B=C	140 U=I	141 Y=C	142 Y=U
143 V=B	144 X=P	145 X=F	146 J=O	147 V=F	148 Z=V
149 N=M	150 O=U	151 T=C	152 J=Y	153 Y=J	154 O=C
155 Z=H	156 K=P	157 H=C	158 K=M	159 B=A	160 B=G
161 W=C	162 S=B	163 H=O	164 B=N	165 O=L	166 S=D
167 F=O	168 Y=C	169 J=D	170 B=M	171 I=R	172 P=K
173 P=B	174 W=K	175 S=W	176 H=D	177 T=G	

Quotes

PAGE/HINT	PAGE/HINT	PAGE/HINT	PAGE/HINT	PAGE/HINT	PAGE/HINT
137 W=D	138 P=F	139 E=R	140 O=P	141 H=F	142 V=R
143 A=K	144 R=S	145 J=H	146 L=C	147 Q=H	148 K=N
149 P=R	150 Q=T	151 J=D	152 A=F	153 Y=O	154 G=D
155 Y=W	156 K=H	157 H=Y	158 B=G	159 E=N	160 V=K
161 O=U	162 I=H	163 B=W	164 U=D	165 X=U	166 Q=P
167 I=B	168 O=C	169 V=D	170 Q=H	171 O=M	172 D=V
173 A=F	174 B=G	175 I=F	176 U=P	177 K=L	

Puzzle Solutions

Crosswords

Sit On It–Page 8

```
A T E M   C H A I R   R U M P
M A X I   P E R S E C U T O R
B U T T   A D R E N A L I N E
S T R   A S I       E R E C T S
    E B B   N A B       A H S
L I M O S     B U G L E
E D I T O R   O N E O N O N E
N E S T L E D   S E C U R E S
S A M O V A R S   K A R A T S
      M E D A L     L E T H E
B E A       B E S   E S O
E X T R A   N I T A     R A P
N I S E I   E G O S   L I M A
C L E A T   S H O T   V E E S
H E A R S   S T L O   I S N T
```

Four Corners–Page 10

```
    S C A T       W H I G
    T E R R A   S H E A R
T H O R E A U   T O R N A D O
R E C T A N G L E S     N E W
I N K   S Q U A R E   M O P E
O N E     U S S     F E L T S
A D R O I T       U T A H
    A P L         C E O
O M N I       C O L O R S
H A I K U     L I L     E C O
A T L   M E X I C O     P O L
D E L     D R I E R   A R E
A R I Z O N A   R A F T I N G
    N O W A Y   O D D E R
    G O E S       O R T S
```

Bit by Bit–Page 9

```
B E G S   R O P E S   V A S E
I N R E   U R I A H   A M E N
T E A M   B A N T U   L A N D
    N I M B L E   T A U N T S
A P T   E E L S   O L A
D E S   T R Y   B U B B L E D
V O T A R Y   B I T   L E N O
E R O S E   B I T   P E A R L
R I M S   B I T   V A S S A L
B A B Y S A T   S A G   E G O
    R E L   P I C A   H E P
R A D I A L   L E A N T O
A B R A   A L E R T   A L E S
G L E N   D E A R E   O D D S
S E W S   S O D A S   S S T S
```

Seven Little Men–Page 11

```
S C H   B A G E L S   F M S
C O O   O R A N G E   F L I T
U N I   N O B L E S   L E T A
B A S H F U L   S N E E Z Y
A N T O I N E S   Y E T I S
    O R D   C O D E
D R I V E   C U B E   G W E N
O N C E   A L L O W   R I V A
C A Y S   D O P E Y   U N I T
    W E P T     S M E L L
H E A V E N   S C A U P
A L B I N O   R E L Y I N G
P L O P   I C I E S T   L E I
P I U S   D O C T O R   S O L
Y E T   S L E E P Y   A N T
```

Crosswords

Nyms–Page 12

```
A L A D   C R A B   O C A L A
M A L I   L O C O   M O R E L
A R E A   O K R A   A L I N E
N A U G H T   O R T H O D O X
A S T R O   E N D E A R
      A N A L Y S T   A T T U
  H O M O N Y M   A U D I O S
B I B   R D S   A N T O N Y M
E D I T S   T A U T   E S C
D E E R   A L I A S E S
      A I D E D   R A I S E
P S E U D O N Y M   S U R E R
A L A M O   T I E S   N O V A
M U S A L   O N L Y   A N E T
D R E S S   S G T S   S Y N O
```

Hi-tech Talk–Page 14

```
C A B   B O S T O N   C P U
A G R   A C C U S E   S L U G
R O E   L E A G U E   N A T L
O R T O L A N   D A I N T Y
M A T R O N S   L I V
      D O S   W H E N E V E R
D E V O N   C O A S T L I N E
I R A   S H U T S   D V D
S T R A I T E N S   O B E Y S
K E Y B O A R D   Q U O
      A L G   A U T O M A T
C A F T A N   L A P T O P S
H I R E   A D A G I O   U P A
A D O S   T I T A N S   S T R
R A M   E M M E T T   E S S
```

Olfactory Sensations–Page 13

```
O D O R   C O M E   F O I S T
W I P E   O P R Y   A R O M A
L A P P   V I S E   T O N E S
    O L S E N   D P T   I L K
S C R I P T E D   R E A C T S
T A T E R   S I T I N S
I N U R E D   S R O   P F C S
N O N   E R A S U R E   R A M
K E E P   I N E   I N S A N E
    S T E N C H   A N G E L
S T A T E S   T E X T U R A L
C O B   R T S   A R E C A
E R O D E   E Z R A   K N O W
N A N A S   N O S Y   U C L A
T H E T A   D E E S   P E E R
```

Rhymes of All Sizes–Page 15

```
R O S Y   A N G L O   F A T
L I M O   L A R G E   T A N K
S L A G   C R E E D   A R G O
    L A H O R E   I D L E R S
P A L   A V O N   P A L S Y
A F B   L E W   F U N D
C R A W L S   H I S   O R C A
K I L O S   F O X   C L E O N
S T L O   T O T   C A L L U S
    D A W G   S O U   A R E
  B A R G E   M E N S   T T L
M A N U A L   O R T E G A
U S A F   V A L V E   A B C D
N A I F   E A T E N   S L A Y
I L L   S H O R T   P E T E
```

181

· Armchair Puzzlers · Solutions ·

Crosswords

Something Fishy–Page 16

B	O	N	O		S	I	N	G		P	E	R	C	H
U	N	I	V			E	M	I	R		A	X	I	O	M
S	O	L	E		T	A	C	O		L	I	O	N	S
		R	R	S		K	U	D	O	S				
S	K	A	T	E		P	E	P	E		T	A	L	E
S	I	N	U	S		A	L	E	C		S	N	A	G
S	N	O	R	E	R	S		R	O	B		T	W	O
		N	T	H			D	E	F				
A	M	P		S	O	B		R	E	A	L	T	O	R
B	A	S	S		M	A	P	S		G	O	O	S	E
E	R	I	C		B	L	O	T		L	U	R	E	D
		E	D	I	C	T		P	E	N			
A	M	I	N	O		O	P	I	E		D	R	A	M
D	E	N	I	M		N	I	L	E		E	A	R	L
D	A	N	C	E		Y	E	L	L		R	P	M	S

Playthings–Page 18

G	A	M	E		A	D	E	S		B	E	S	T	S
A	M	E	N		B	A	L	L		E	N	T	R	E
G	I	R	L		A	P	S	E		F	L	O	U	R
	C	A	T	C	H		D	S	O		V	C	R
B	L	U	R	R	I	N	G		E	U	R	E	K	A
L	A	R	G	E		E	A	S	E	L	S		
O	R	I	E	N	T		S	I	S		T	A	R	A
O	V	A		D	I	P		P	T	S		M	O	B
M	A	L	L		R	E	G		O	C	C	U	P	Y
		S	C	A	R	A	B		R	O	S	E	S
A	B	S	U	R	D		B	L	U	E	N	E	S	S
T	O	Y		E	E	R		O	P	E	C		
B	U	R	M	A		E	T	C	S		E	L	M	O
A	L	U	M	S		B	I	K	E		D	O	L	L
T	E	P	E	E		A	S	S	T		E	N	I	D

Scores–Page 17

A	E	I	O		P	I	N		R	O	A	D	S
S	P	O	N	S	O	R	E	D		U	P	S	E	T
T	O	U	C	H	D	O	W	N		N	E	H	R	U
I	S	S	U	E		N	S	A		R	E	N	D
		E	S	S			E	R	A			
C	P	A		S	T	R	I	K	E		O	S	U
R	O	L	L		R	O	O	S	E	V	E	L	T	S
A	L	L	I	E		R	S	T		S	P	A	R	E
F	I	E	L	D	G	O	A	L	S		A	F	A	R
T	O	Y		N	A	S	S	E	R		S	Y	S
		G	A	A	P			O	U	T		
G	O	A	L		A	L	E		N	O	T	S	O
A	R	T	E	S		M	A	R	T	I	N	E	T	S
S	C	O	R	E		P	O	I	N	T		A	L	L
H	A	R	T	E			S	E	T	S		R	O	O

Who Let 'Em Out?–Page 19

I	D	Y	L		A	P	E	S		C	O	B	R	A
S	E	E	A		D	O	L	E		O	R	L	O	N
T	A	L	C		L	O	F	T		R	O	U	G	E
	L	U	C	I	D		H	A	G		F	U	N
A	T	O	N	A	B	L	E		M	I	F	F	E	D
R	O	W	A	N		E	R	N	E	S	T		
C	O	L	L	I	E		I	A	L		C	C	C	P
E	R	A		S	C	O	T	T	I	E		H	O	E
D	A	B	S		O	R	R		A	M	B	E	R	S
		A	S	L	E	E	P		B	U	R	N	T
B	E	A	G	L	E		A	U	R	E	L	I	U	S
O	Y	L		A	S	H		P	U	R	L	S		
D	R	I	L	L		A	V	I	D		D	H	O	W
E	I	E	I	O		L	I	L	Y		O	E	N	O
D	E	N	I	M		T	E	S	S		G	R	I	N

182

Crosswords

Subjects–Page 20

```
BAIT  STAGE  MATH
BANE  TITAN  OLIO
CASE  UNRIG  NOME
   ONEDGE  LEONES
GYM  PILE  INTER
LON  EEE  OSLO
ARISES  SCH  NUTS
REAPS  UPS  NITRO
ESSE  SKY  SOCIAL
   LICE  TUB  LII
 DALAI  AONE  IND
SALINE  BALLOT
ECON  NORSE  AIDE
CHUG  CHATS  HEIR
TAD  EMMYS  USNA
```

Classical Puns–Page 22

```
ABA  ILL  ETHICAL
MALARIA  GROCERY
ACTRESS  GENERAL
SHOP  ZSA  NESTLE
   UTILITY
TOGAS  ELM  BOSS
BARBER  PRAIRIE
ORIOLE  HANDEL
NEEDED  COR  EVE
EDGES  AHA  OGRES
   SIDELINE
BEER  HAYDN  NAPS
ANTIWAR  RUPTURE
ROULADE  ORE  ROE
SLIER  NET  ASK
```

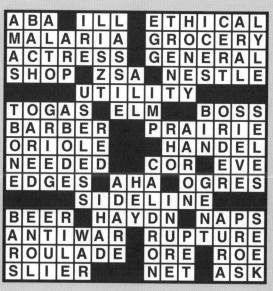

The "Spices" of Life–Page 21

```
ASHE  BLOB  BABAR
SPIT  OGRE  ATONE
SALT  WEED  SMOTE
ORDERS  GOBI  MEL
CEASE  BAUBLE
   CLINIC  ATOM
HAL  EATON  DRAMA
ELPASO  PEPPER
REGIS  SPOON  ANT
BEAR  STANDS
   SPHERE  ERASE
FDA  AYES  ERECTS
LILAC  PLAN  TIES
ALACK  LEWD  IDEA
PLIES  EYES  ESPY
```

7 Cs–Page 23

```
COL  COMETO  MOB
SPA  URANUS  HERR
IRR  LATENS  ITSA
CAVEATS  IGLOOS
KHARTOUM  FELONS
   NER  OMITS
STAIR  KNEES  EYE
EAVE  WAKES  CRED
APE  CARET  BURNS
   DAILY  SET
SCRIPT  CINGIDOG
NAUSEA  SIGNIFY
OINK  NEVADA  ATP
URNS  DRAWER  NES
TOY  CSTARS  ANY
```

Crosswords

Picture This–Page 24

```
NEGS  SLAV  PEDAL
ANNE  NONO  HAILE
ALAE  AWAY  ORCAS
CATSUP TACTLESS
PISAN  NOGOOD
      WISEMEN OVER
FIT SHAY CAMERA
IRONOUT HOTSEAT
LATENT SUCH SSE
MEOW  TAUNTER
      SPELLS NACHO
BACCARAT SACRED
UBOAT SAPS HALO
FLASH KNOT EVER
FELTS ASPS LENS
```

Opposites Attract–Page 26

```
SHOE  SWEET  BABE
COLD  OILER  AWRY
ITIS  USURY  LAIR
  GEARED  ONSIDE
STALL  EDUCATE
ARR FAT ETO
BACKACHES SHORT
ACHE  HICKS  ARIA
EYE  ONO  THRILL
   PRO LURE GEL
LISA PEP ACID
SERAPHS  SEDAN
COOK  OATHS  MAIM
ANNE  SLOOP  ELLA
NESS  EMPTY  OSLO
```

Lazy English–Page 25

```
ALDA  NITE  OSCAR
AUDI  ARID  VAULT
AVER  MENU  AMPLE
   SSE  SCALP
GOTTA  REAP  LITE
ADORN  ALTO  ECHO
BEWITCH  ELS  HON
   PAR    LAG
AIM SIS LOVABLE
XMAS  STEP  ALIGN
EARP  PALS  GAZED
   HASNT  SEC
COVER  DORA  THRU
UNARM  BRIG  IMET
ZONES  YODA  COPE
```

Barnyard Sounds–Page 27

```
ETTE  HATED  MEOW
WOOF  OCHRE  ARIA
EARL  ORION  RAND
  MASTERS  BASKS
SEETHE  DILATES
ERN ARF OPAH
MOTELS  RNS  ONCE
IDONT  LES  SNELL
SERF  TAD  MISCUE
   OPEN CAT ECG
 SPREADS  RIMSKY
QUACK  LATINOS
URGE  IOWAN  TAMS
AGAR  CRETE  EROS
YENS  UDDER  LYON
```

Crosswords

Rhyming Words–Page 28

C	R	I	B		T	I	M	E		T	H	Y	M	E
L	A	N	E		H	O	A	X		R	O	W	E	R
I	D	E	A		O	U	C	H		O	S	C	A	R
M	I	R	R	O	R		H	A	B	I	T	A	T	S
B	I	T	E	S		P	I	L	O	S	E			
			R	A	V	I	N	E	S		L	I	M	E
A	T	E		G	E	N	E		W	A	R	R	E	D
S	I	A	M	E	S	E		R	E	L	Y	I	N	G
A	T	R	E	S	T		M	A	L	L		S	U	E
P	O	N	G		I	C	I	C	L	E	S			
			A	R	G	O	S	Y		G	O	R	G	E
M	I	S	D	O	E	R	S		G	E	N	E	R	A
I	D	I	O	M		D	I	M	E		A	L	I	S
M	E	N	S	A		E	L	B	A		T	A	M	E
E	S	S	E	N		R	E	A	R		A	X	E	L

Space Race–Page 29

C	L	U	B		O	N	M	E		S	P	A	D	E
L	U	N	A		P	E	E	L		E	R	R	E	D
A	R	C	S		T	O	R	T		R	O	A	L	D
R	E	L	I	C	S		C	O	L	U	M	B	I	A
A	D	E	L	A		A	U	R	U	M				
			M	A	T	R	O	N		A	B	A	S	
D	A	W		E	M	M	Y		A	S	P	E	C	T
A	P	O	L	L	O			I	T	E	R	A	T	E
I	S	L	E	S		S	T	O	I	C		M	I	R
S	O	F	A		S	P	E	N	C	E	R			
			F	L	O	U	R	S		D	A	V	I	D
I	B	M		I	N	T	R		G	E	M	I	N	I
L	O	A	F	S		N	A	M	E		B	C	D	E
S	O	Y	U	Z		I	C	O	N		L	A	I	T
A	B	O	R	T		K	E	P	T		E	R	A	S

Give Me A Sign–Page 30

I	S	E	E		A	S	A	P		A	W	F	U	L
A	L	L	Y		B	I	D	E		G	R	I	P	E
N	Y	S	E		B	R	E	D		R	A	B	I	D
			T	O	Y		X	M	A	S				
C	A	M	E	L		O	H	I	O		S	L	O	W
O	I	L	E	D		R	U	N	G		E	I	R	E
T	R	I	T	E		B	B	G	U	N		D	E	B
			H	S	T			L	O	T				
U	S	S		T	I	D	E	S		R	U	R	A	L
S	T	O	P		M	E	S	S		M	E	R	G	E
C	U	B	A		E	A	T	S		A	S	S	E	T
			N	E	R	D		L	L	D				
G	R	E	E	D		E	T	T	A		A	T	O	P
Y	I	E	L	D		N	O	R	M		Y	A	L	E
M	O	S	S	Y		D	R	I	P		S	O	D	A

185

Moored Homonyms–Page 31

S	A	N	T	A		A	C	M	E		W	E	F	T
T	H	O	R	N		I	H	O	P		O	L	L	A
L	I	V	I	D		R	A	T	E		R	I	A	L
			P	O	L	Y	T	H	E	I	S	T	I	C
A	D	S		R	I	A		S	I	S	T	E	R	S
R	E	A	L	R	E	E	L		S	E	W			
M	E	D	I	A		R	I	O	T	O	U	S	L	Y
E	R	A	T		P	I	O	U	S		R	H	E	E
D	E	T	E	R	R	E	N	T		A	S	I	A	N
			R	E	O		S	W	E	E	T	E	S	T
A	T	L	A	N	T	A		I	S	R		D	E	L
B	E	T	T	E	R	B	E	T	T	O	R			
A	N	C	E		A	N	E	T		B	I	N	G	O
C	O	O	L		C	E	R	E		I	D	E	A	L
I	N	L	Y		T	R	O	D		C	E	A	S	E

Crosswords

More Moored Homonyms–Page 32

```
A R A B   B A R E   R O B O T
B O L A   E L E M   E P O X Y
O D I N   A S A P   S T R E P
M E A N E R   D I V E   N N E
B O R E D   H E R E T O
    D E M U R E R   G O B I
B M W   M I S S   B A R R E N
E Y E L A S H   V E T E R A N
E R N E S T   A I N T   S T S
T A T A   A B S T A I N
    D A K O T A   R E A R S
A C T   G E A R   B E E P E R
B A R O N   R O M A   D R A T
C R U D E   D I O N   L I R A
S L E D S   D I D   E L M S
```

Pot of Gold–Page 34

```
B L U E   B U R R   S O N G S
M E S A   A N O A   A R I E L
W E A R   H O Y T   M A L T Y
    T V S   G R E E N
S U S H I   E B A N   G L O W
R A D I O   V I C E   E A S E
O R I E L   E V E R Y   P U B
    R E D       O E D
G N P   T R A D E   L I S P S
Y E T I   A R E A   L A K E S
M O A N   M A S T   O M I T S
    D E A L T   T W O
C U P I D   S I T E   N A D A
I M A G E   E N I D   D R U M
A P R O N   A Y E S   S C O T
```

Entertaining Awards–Page 33

```
W O M B   T O N Y   N O B E L
A L E E   A S I A   O P E R A
R I C H   S U P P O S E D L Y
M O H A W K   T E N S E S
    A L E   E S S O
P E N F A U L K N E R   T S E
A L I   R A D I O   E N A C T
R O C   I R E   W A N   I R A
S P A I N   R A M I E   L U G
E E L   G O L D E N G L O B E
    L Y O N   E E R
E A T I N G   G R A M M Y
T H E R E A F T E R   D A R E
O S C A R   I O L A   E D E N
N O S E D   E M M Y   R E D S
```

Original Evil Spirits–Page 35

```
A L A I   A G R I   T U F T S
L E H R   D I E D   E N U R E
I A M A   A N G E   M E N U S
B R A N D Y   R A M P A G E S
I N D I A   M E T E O R
    S P O T T E D   N O D E
E B B   P A N S   I B E R I A
R E E F E R S   W A R D E N S
S M E A R S   N I T A   S O Y
E A R N   M E A N E S T
    A V E N U E   S I E G E
I C E T O N G S   C Y G N E T
S O L I D   A E R O   E D N A
T R A C K   G A U L   R O O T
S A L S A   E S M E   S R A S
```

Crosswords

Day Starters–Page 36

```
JUICE  EBBS  ORGS
ILIAD  YEAH  BALI
BEING  ENCE  ICAN
   SIMP  ORATING
ASP EPI  NIL  ACE
THRUSHES  FABLE
TOAST  COFFEE
YETI  BELLS  AMIR
  NAUSEA  ASIDE
 PAGES  STARTLES
ALF RIP UNA  KAT
MUFFINS  LAME
BRIE  EYRE  AGATE
LARD  SCAN  IGLOO
ELMS  SHUT  CSPAN
```

Colorful Rhymes–Page 38

```
HIGH  ASTER   GPA
AWRY  WHITE  BLEW
POEM  AIMED  LEAN
  ENDIVE  HAUNTS
OWN  RTES  EVENS
FOB  AER  JAGS
FOETID  POD  HOSS
ALAIN  MAE  TORII
LYNN  BET  HOEING
  KHAN  SAW  GUM
 BREST  SHIN  ISA
ALERTS  PERSON
PAVE  MARIN  JACK
SCUD  ALIKE  ALAI
EKE  NIGHT  ISNT
```

Portals–Page 37

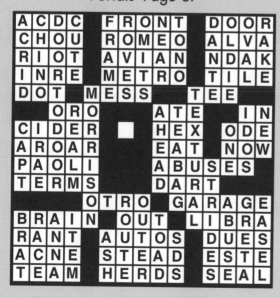

```
ACDC  FRONT  DOOR
CHOU  ROMEO  ALVA
RIOT  AVIAN  NDAK
INRE  METRO  TILE
DOT  MESS  TEE
 ORO   ATE   IN
CIDER   HEX  ODE
AROAR  EAT  NOW
PAOLI  ABUSES
TERMS  DART
  OTRO  GARAGE
BRAIN  OUT  LIBRA
RANT  AUTOS  DUES
ACNE  STEAD  ESTE
TEAM  HERDS  SEAL
```

Geometric Homonyms–Page 39

```
AMAD  SENSE  THEM
NAME  PLAIN  AERO
SUPS  HUMBLENESS
WRECKED  ANGLES
EIRE  REM  IDE
REENFORCE  NEON
  TRI  SAP  TAPE
SIR YDS TAP  RTE
ACES  SIP  SID
CULL  CONSTENTS
  UAW  DIP  SEEA
ISOMER  COSIGNS
STEPSISTER  RAES
LONE  TOAST  ETTE
APOD  EXITS  SESS
```

187

Crosswords

Second Grade Homonyms–Page 40

```
T E A   U N S A F E     S C H
A L T   N O T I O N   H E R E
M M E   C R I M E S   A N E W
P E A F O W L     E S T A T E
A R R I V A L S   N E S T E D
      N E Y   W E A R
O N A I R   H E A D F I R S T
F E E T   R E A T A   T U T U
F O R E B E A R S   W H E R E
      A C R E   R I A
T H E Y R E   R A I N C O A T
H E R O E S   M O N A R C H
E N I D   S E N A T E   R O E
I N C A   E A S T E R   I R R
R A S   S T A I R S   N N E
```

Night-Night–Page 42

```
S L E E P     D R E A M
N E W E R     E A T N O
O V I N E     W I T C H
R E N   P Y A   S E E R
E R G   E S S E S
      N I G H T
M A L I N G E R   B E D
A D O L F   I N U R E
R E N E E   A C R E S
E S E   R H E T O R I C
      N O S E S
P I L L O W S   P J S
I D E A   S E A   E A T
L E A C H   D R A P E
L A S E R   M A C A W
S L E D S   S T E N S
```

Bonds–Page 41

```
S P A D   B O S C   M O O R E
P A B A   O L E O   O M A H A
O P A L   N E L L   R I T E S
R U S T L E   L O N G S H O T
T A H O E   C E N S U S
      N A D I R   F E I G N S
O D E   R E T S     O R E O
L A Z E N B Y   C O N N E R Y
E R R A T A   B A B Y   G O A
G N A T   C A R R E L
      E L L I O T   O R S O N
B A R R I E R S   S N E E Z E
A V O I D   I N S T   T W O S
N O T E S   N A M E   R E N T
E W E S   G N U S   O R E S
```

All Good Things–Page 43

```
T Y P O   A S S T S   F O B
W O R M   S T O R E   A L V A
A N O N   P A P U A   B E A D
    F I N I S H   F I N A L E
E M E   U R I S   O N O
L E S   D I S   C O E R C E
E N S I G N   E N D   M O N T
C L O S E   P A N   B A N J O
T O R T   C A R   F A L C O N
      A I L S   B I S   L Y E
B U N C O   C A L I   U S S
A I R B U S   A L L E Y S
E S A U   U N C L E   A I R S
R O L L   R O T O R   L O O T
O N S   E D I T S   E N D S
```

188

· Armchair Puzzlers · Solutions ·

Crosswords

Bad Jokes–Page 44

U	T	A	H		I	D	E	S		B	L	O	N	D
M	E	G	A		N	U	L	L		L	A	M	A	R
P	A	R	I		D	E	L	A		O	B	E	S	E
	E	R	W	I	N		M	A	N		G	A	S	
E	L	E	P	H	A	N	T		I	D	E	A	L	S
M	A	M	I	E		A	I	R	M	E	N			
O	P	E	N	E	R		D	Y	E		T	U	R	N
T	I	N		L	A	W	Y	E	R	S		N	E	O
E	S	T	H		C	H	I		S	A	C	H	E	M
			A	S	I	A	N	S		L	H	A	S	A
A	N	T	I	C	S		G	O	S	S	I	P	E	D
B	A	R		O	M	B		N	A	A	C	P		
O	N	I	O	N		R	O	A	D		K	I	L	T
U	N	C	L	E		I	O	T	A		E	L	I	E
T	Y	K	E	S		T	H	A	T		N	Y	P	D

Snappy Comebacks–Page 46

D	O	N	T		N	O	T	I		W	O	O	D	Y
A	H	A	B		A	S	O	N		I	N	D	I	A
N	A	N	O		B	U	L	B		P	E	D	A	L
C	R	A	N	E	S		S	O	R	E		S	S	E
E	A	S	E	D		A	T	R	E	S	T			
			S	I	P	H	O	N	S		A	S	T	I
I	S	R		B	U	O	Y		P	I	N	T	O	S
S	H	I	R	L	E	Y		P	E	N	G	U	I	N
E	A	S	I	E	R		P	E	L	T		B	L	T
E	D	E	N		I	C	I	C	L	E	S			
			G	U	L	A	G	S		R	O	G	E	R
N	U	T	S	H	E	L	L		U	N	D	O	N	E
A	N	A	I	L		L	E	A	R		I	O	T	A
P	A	N	D	A		M	T	N	S		U	S	E	D
E	S	S	E	N		E	S	T	A		M	E	R	E

Horsin' Around–Page 45

F	A	L	S	E		L	O	R	E		S	A	V	E
E	P	S	O	M		A	D	I	N		E	C	A	D
B	L	U	R	B		K	O	N	G		A	T	L	I
		T	A	T	E	R	S		A	B	O	U	T	
E	K	E		R	O	B		E	M	P	I	R	E	S
M	O	N	O	G	R	A	M		A	B	S			
M	A	R	C	O		G	U	R	U		C	A	M	E
A	L	O	E		P	E	R	I	L		U	N	I	V
S	A	L	A		S	L	A	V		S	I	N	C	E
			N	O	S		L	E	F	T	T	U	R	N
A	G	I	T	A	T	E		R	B	I		L	O	T
T	A	R	O	T		L	Y	R	I	C	S			
S	T	O	A		C	L	E	O		K	O	R	E	A
E	O	N	S		S	I	L	L		E	D	I	C	T
A	S	S	T		T	E	L	L		R	A	N	G	E

The Twain Shall Meet–Page 47

P	A	M	P	A		H	E	F	T		T	S	P	S
S	C	A	L	P		E	L	L	S		H	E	R	A
S	C	O	U	R		A	L	A	E		E	R	A	T
			S	I	E	V	E	S		A	C	I	D	Y
E	S	T		O	L	E		H	E	L	L	F	O	R
N	E	U	T	R	I	N	O		A	S	I			
D	E	L	H	I		F	U	L	S	O	M	E		
S	A	S	E		R	O	S	I	E		A	Q	U	A
		A	S	S	E	R	T	S		U	T	U	R	N
			O	P	A		S	T	O	N	E	A	G	E
C	O	N	C	E	R	T		E	S	C		L	E	W
A	V	O	I	D		R	A	N	S	O	M			
D	I	M	E		M	I	M	I		V	I	P	E	R
G	N	A	T		D	A	M	N		E	L	O	P	E
E	E	N	Y		S	L	O	G		R	E	D	I	D

· Armchair Puzzlers · Solutions ·

Crosswords

Why?—Page 48

G	E	T		■	S	P	E	W	■	H	E	A	R	T
A	V	E	S	■	A	R	E	A	■	A	R	L	E	S
P	A	R	K	■	D	E	L	L	■	W	A	L	L	A
■	R	U	R	A	L	■	K	I	A	■	E	E	R	■
P	H	O	N	E	T	I	C	■	G	I	A	N	T	S
L	A	R	K	S	■	M	A	R	L	I	N	■	■	■
A	R	I	S	T	O	■	S	A	O	■	D	R	U	G
I	T	S	■	■	D	I	T	T	O	S	■	E	P	A
T	E	M	P	■	E	N	L	■	S	T	E	N	O	S
■	■	■	I	N	S	T	E	P	■	O	V	E	N	S
R	A	N	G	E	S	■	D	R	I	V	E	W	A	Y
A	D	E	■	W	A	Y	■	O	P	E	R	A	■	■
B	L	O	A	T	■	E	M	M	A	■	E	B	B	S
B	I	N	G	O	■	A	M	P	S	■	S	L	U	G
I	B	S	E	N	■	R	E	T	S	■	T	E	N	T

190

Word Puzzles
Solutions

Word Puzzles

Page 51

Word Muddles
ANIMAL TALK
drca kshra = card shark
iapbggkcy = piggyback
nnheimseoky = monkeyshine
lawkatc = catwalk
bdri aribn = bird brain
aidrblji = jailbird
oohepinegl = pigeonhole
owikclc = cowlick
kcbal peseh = black sheep
blulrdoez = bulldozer

Page 52

Before & After
Al Gore Vidal Sassoon
Andy Dick Clark Gable

Letter Shuffle
TYPES OF TREES
Elm, Fir, Beech, Oak, Palm

Page 53

Antonym Word Search
Anagrams
PLEBAIL = PLIABLE
IFLECA = FACILE
OYRSMT = STORMY
TOYLSC = COSTLY
BEIVLIS = VISIBLE
NARDAIT = RADIANT

Antonyms
RIGID
HARD
CALM
CHEAP
HIDDEN
DULL

Antonym Word Search

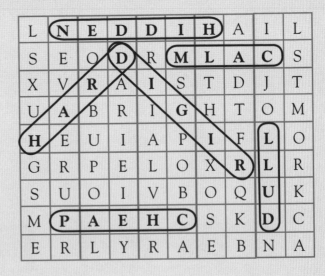

It Takes Two

Word Puzzles

Antonym Word Search

Y	R	E	T	S	Y	M	X	G	Y
X	O	A	J	X	A	S	M	N	N
D	T	S	S	I	M	E	R	I	G
E	N	I	E	L	C	D	W	V	J
V	W	O	U	D	R	L	D	I	O
A	O	L	A	G	U	R	F	G	E
U	N	P	F	I	U	R	S	H	B
S	K	C	O	M	Q	U	C	D	E
N	R	A	B	Y	K	C	U	L	N

It Takes Two

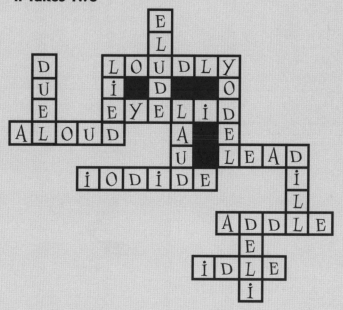

193

Word Puzzles

Page 56
Acrostic Part 1
A) Racketeer   B) Goatee
C) Whiten   D) Filing
E) Tiniest   F) Wonderland
G) Novelist   H) Hiawatha
I) Swedish   J) Twin
K) Whig   L) Tint

Page 57
Acrostic Part 2
"What I want I take if I can get it, and so I wrestle neither with angels nor devils."
Gone with the Wind
(by Margaret Mitchell)

Page 58
Acrostic Part 1
A) Bewilder   B) Entrance
C) Honeymoon   D) Tedious
E) Seasonal   F) Mayan
G) Toad   H) Yacht
I) Advantage   J) Nonfat
K) Yellowish   L) Oat

Page 59
Acrostic Part 2
"Maybe you'd go away and never call, and a taste of honey is worse than none at all."
"I Second That Emotion"
(by Smokey Robinson)

Page 60
Word Muddles
HAPPY CAMPERS
erfmaicp = campfire
lssaawmhorlm = marshmallows
kkcabcap = backpack
hgfihsllat = flashlight
seomrs = smores
nrlnate = lantern
eplnreetl = repellent
itotle eprap = toilet paper
rltia ixm = trail mix
pocsmas = compass

Page 61
Word Muddles
HOT LUNCH
ckciehn irnsfeg = chicken fingers
trato stot = tator tots
teolamfa = meatloaf
zpzai = pizza
gbesruecehre = cheeseburger
ghspeitat = spaghetti
rdilegl seceeh = grilled cheese
lgsaana = lasagna
rongcsdo = corndogs
altsaemlb = meatballs

Page 62
Before & After
George Harrison Ford
Eli Whitney Houston
Raul Julia Child

Letter Shuffle
ROYAL TITLES
King, Queen, Prince, Duke, Count

194

Word Puzzles

Page 63

Antonym Word Search
Anagrams

YESCATS = ECSTASY
EVIBEEL = BELIEVE
EDITCE = DECEIT
OHMSOT = SMOOTH
CLEATO = LOCATE
HFALYS = FLASHY

Antonyms
DISGUST
DOUBT
TRUTH
ROUGH
MISLAY
PLAIN

Antonym Word Search

O	T	S	U	G	S	I	D	G	Y
H	S	I	L	E	R	N	J	I	E
G	H	Z	P	L	A	I	N	N	T
U	S	H	G	X	Y	M	U	B	A
O	H	T	B	E	T	L	U	Q	H
R	O	U	D	I	J	O	L	T	D
M	W	R	T	S	D	P	R	N	L
V	Y	T	Y	A	L	S	I	M	E
A	R	L	C	F	U	I	Z	E	R

It Takes Two

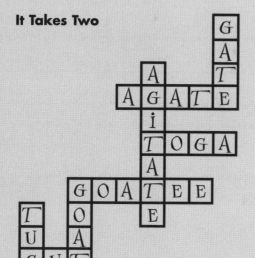

Page 64

Before & After
Bob Dylan Thomas
Hank Aaron Burr
Randy Travis Tritt

Letter Shuffle
FARM ANIMALS
Sheep, Horse, Pig,
Goose, Rooster

Word Puzzles

Page 65

Antonym Word Search
Anagrams
CANNITE = ANCIENT
RTYDA = TARDY
ANYTHUG = NAUGHTY
REVPITA = PRIVATE
FOICRMN = CONFIRM
SLAYCS = CLASSY

Antonyms
RECENT
PROMPT
NICE
PUBLIC
DENY
TACKY

It Takes Two

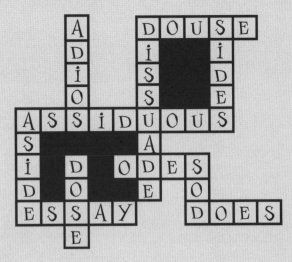

Antonym Word Search

Page 66

Acrostic Part 1
A) Barnacle   B) Wingding
C) Harbinger   D) Latke
E) Knell   F) Shallot
G) Oleander   H) Sheath
I) Boss   J) Freshest
K) Bowed   L) Whet

Page 67

Acrostic Part 2
"Renewed shall be blade that was
broken, the crownless again shall
be King." *The Lord of the Rings*
(by J.R.R. Tolkien)

Word Puzzles

Page 68

Acrostic Part 1
A) Conga

B) Gnome

C) Hyena

D) Fashion

E) Shredder

F) Honor

G) Tofu

H) Fauna

I) Yahoo

J) Tattle

K) Sashes

L) Oast

M) Mako

N) Beer

Page 69

Acrostic Part 2
"You can shake the hand of the mango man as he greets you at the border." "Son of a Son of a Sailor" (by Jimmy Buffett)

Page 70

Word Muddles
ANCHORS AWAY

taablosi = sailboat

baecarln = barnacle

cbnia = cabin

pcaitan = captain

dinyhg = dinghy

yaellg = galley

oochesnr = schooner

rcsyuv = scurvy

hytca = yacht

ouagbtt = tugboat

Page 71

Word Muddles
"C" FOOD DIET

arcosrt = carrots

earlce = cereal

radceem oncr = creamed corn

eaauocnltp = cantaloupe

ekoioc = cookie

udrstac = custard

prcee = crepe

ecsresola = casserole

roatnssic = croissant

rclfiwluoae = cauliflower

Page 72

Before & After
Lenny Bruce Lee Marvin Gaye

Letter Shuffle
FOREST ANIMALS

Bear, Deer, Elk, Fox, Badger

Word Puzzles

Page 73

Antonym Word Search
Anagrams
CADROW = COWARD
FLIPUT = UPLIFT
DINKDER = KINDRED
HBGRIT = BRIGHT
RETCROC = CORRECT
UCAUVSO = VACUOUS

Antonyms
HERO
LOWER
ALIEN
DARK
FALSE
FILLED

It Takes Two

Page 74

Before & After
Etta James Dean Martin Sheen

Letter Shuffle
ANIMAL SOUNDS
Moo, Bark, Oink, Quack, Neigh

Antonym Word Search

Word Puzzles

Page 75

Antonym Word Search
Anagrams
IPLEOT = POLITE
RIMGNAT = MIGRANT
STNUJU = UNJUST
AECLNC = CANCEL
AVENI = NAÏVE
SOYIN = NOISY

Antonyms
RUDE
IDLE
FAIR
RENEW
JADED
QUIET

It Takes Two

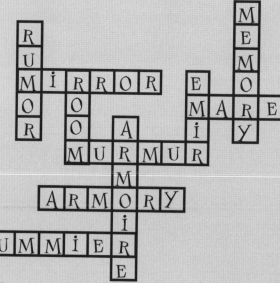

Antonym Word Search

Word Puzzles

Page 76
Acrostic Part 1
A) Fleece
B) West Indies
C) Slingshot
D) Ostrich
E) Doubloon
F) Monthly
G) Wharf
H) Heartburn
I) Weapon
J) Matthew
K) Fountain
L) Spindrift
M) No one
N) Acme

Page 77
Acrostic Part 2
"The amount of women in London who flirt with their own husbands is perfectly scandalous."
The Importance of Being Earnest
(by Oscar Wilde)

Page 78
Acrostic Part 1
A) Overheats
B) Troll
C) Surfboard
D) Plod
E) Lavished
F) Sahara
G) Formaldehyde
H) Faint
I) Dill
J) Deodorant
K) Shareholder
L) Reserve
M) Cassette

Page 79
Acrostic Part 2
"She drives real fast and she drives real hard. She's the terror of Colorado Boulevard." "The Little Old Lady from Pasadena"
(by The Beach Boys)

Page 80
Word Muddles
LIFE'S A BEACH
sveloh = shovel
lasetc = castle
teolw = towel
mulblrea = umbrella
srhtsaif = starfish
snstue = sunset
ewasede = seaweed
rdfiualeg = lifeguard
einseholr = shoreline
kdroalwba = boardwalk

Page 81
Word Muddles
MUSEUM MILE
uvlroe = Louvre
roapd = Prado
itmloteporna = Metropolitan
zfiiuf = Uffizi
natvcia = Vatican
amtiehger = Hermitage
ttea = Tate
teygt = Getty
omudo = Duomo
igngeemuhg = Guggenheim

Page 82
Before & After
Connie Francis Marion Jones
Victor Hugo Wolf Blitzer

Letter Shuffle
COLORS
Red, Yellow, Black, Brown, Green

Word Puzzles

Page 83

Antonym Word Search
Anagrams
GAEVU = VAGUE
DEECPER = PRECEDE
WRYSOD = DROWSY
NICEMOB = COMBINE
IITDM = TIMID
THECAD = DETACH

Antonyms
CLEAR
FOLLOW
ALERT
DIVIDE
BOLD
AFFIX

It Takes Two

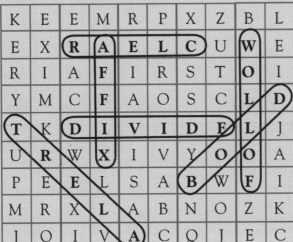

Antonym Word Search

Word Puzzles

Page 84

Before & After
Garry Marshall Mathers
Jennie Garth Brooks
John Wayne Newton

Letter Shuffle
THINGS TO WEAR
Shirt, Coat, Shoes, Socks, Jeans

Page 85

Antonym Word Search
Anagrams
OROISEUFC = FEROCIOUS
TDCEIRIN = INDIRECT
SRMTA = SMART
LAEEV = LEAVE
ITMOS = MOIST

Antonyms
TAME
UPFRONT
DUMB
RETURN
ARID

It Takes Two

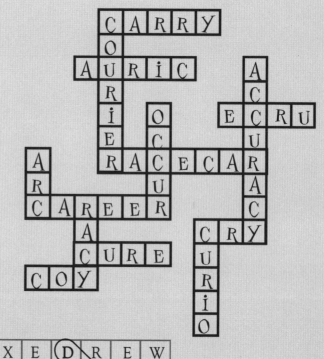

Antonym Word Search

Word Puzzles

Page 86

Acrostic Part 1
A) Document
B) Ladybug
C) Thin ice
D) Statehouses
E) Vacationist
F) Orchestra
G) Rhinestone
H) Fragment
I) Hometown
J) Gearshift
K) Aria
L) Teeth
M) Anathema

Page 87

Acrostic Part 2
"It was a matter of chance that I should have rented a house in one of the strangest communities in North America."
The Great Gatsby
(by F. Scott Fitzgerald)

Page 88

Acrostic Part 1
A) Manifest
B) Tiger
C) Pigeon
D) Knight
E) Pygmy
F) Afterglow
G) Shingle
H) Easel
I) Determine
J) Anciently
K) Initially
L) Gain

Page 89

Acrostic Part 2
"Taking my time, lying there and staring at the ceiling, waiting for a sleepy feeling."
"I'm Only Sleeping"
(by The Beatles)

Page 90

Word Muddles
IT'S NOT EASY BEING GREEN
anebs = beans
asgrs = grass
imktre = Kermit
gllatioar = alligator
gtian = giant
veelas = leaves
lrcocbio = broccoli
mesil = slime
tctleue = lettuce
oscrmkah = shamrock

Page 91

Word Muddles
IT'S A ZOO OUT THERE
riglola = gorilla
inlo = lion
riteg = tiger
anheeplt = elephant
rabez = zebra
kroanoga = kangaroo
reaigff = giraffe
npgneiu = penguin
telaneop = antelope
omagilfn = flamingo

Page 92

Before & After
Johnny Carson Daly
Muhammad Ali MacGraw
Spike Lee Cobb

Letter Shuffle
HEAD HUNT
Tooth, Ear, Eye, Nose, Chin

203

Word Puzzles

Page 93

Antonym Word Search
Anagrams
ELRSSHMA = HARMLESS
ONSNYMY = SYNONYM
RAITCC = ARCTIC
ESWTE = SWEET
BSMROE = SOMBER

Antonyms
RISKY
ANTONYM
TROPICAL
ACERBIC
COMICAL

Antonym Word Search

It Takes Two

Page 94

Before & After
Andrew Jackson Browne
Kobe Bryant Gumbel
Jason Alexander Bell

Letter Shuffle
BUGS
Flea, Ant, Mite, Roach, Tick

Word Puzzles

Page 95

Antonym Word Search
Anagrams
ARISENEC = INCREASE
NGOYU = YOUNG
HOSOMT = SMOOTH
UMFAOS = FAMOUS
LMPETIOI = IMPOLITE

Antonyms
DECREASE
MATURE
ROUGH
OBSCURE
CIVIL

Antonym Word Search

X	C	F	R	L	O	O	R	P	R
O	A	J	Y	H	I	L	E	O	E
L	T	R	A	M	H	V	L	B	H
P	C	O	G	E	A	R	I	S	E
A	T	U	M	Z	O	T	O	C	I
I	S	G	I	A	L	H	U	U	C
Y	F	H	W	C	P	W	I	R	L
E	S	A	E	R	C	E	D	E	E
A	Z	L	N	A	M	R	B	A	Y

It Takes Two

```
E L A T E
i
L O O T
T     U
      L   A L T O
      L     L
      T E A L
L O T T O
      i
      L A T T E
```

Word Puzzles

Page 96

Acrostic Part 1
A) Navigate	B) Crunchy
C) Pogo	D) Rice
E) Terrify	F) Morsel
G) Faded	H) Informal
I) Celery	J) Demonstrate
K) Howled	L) Lymph
M) Ramen	N) Divan

Page 97

Acrostic Part 2
"I'm a lone lorn creature myself, and everything has gone contrary with me from my cradle."
David Copperfield (by Charles Dickens)

Page 98

Word Muddles
FAMOUS MONKEYS
uiuocrs egorge = Curious George
bnooz = Bonzo
ingk gokn = King Kong
sbebulb = Bubbles
prega pea = Grape Ape
carlem = Marcel
noihhmchci = Monchhichi
ikrfai = Rafiki
pzipy = Zippy
gikn eluio = King Louie
ebra = Bear

Word Searches
Solutions

Word Searches

SUNDAE SCHOOL Page 100

```
R Y R R E H C Q K G B T E Z E
E G B T A O C H C N U R C F L
E R C O C B O M J B T N U M P
F J L O Q A O L R Y T S A J U
F F N R V N L O J Q E E S T A
O U S T R A W B E R R I E S E
T S D E Y N H W G C S K L R N
O E N A I A I P D A C O K A I
W I O E J S P E U R O O N E P
A M M G Z E P C F A T C I B Y
L M L F A P Y A T M C E R Y Z
N I A N I U D N O E H Y P M J
U J U H S T N S H L L V S M B
T T W O L L A M H S R A M U P
S D X Q F N C P M L B Q V G P
```

MOOD FOR THOUGHT Page 101

```
M F S S D S A Q E W C G A A J
W F D Q L Q T O O E H A N G H
Q T N E I T A P M I J X G V P
R C E U P H O R I C I F R E U
O P A L Z R I G L O O M Y A G
Y V A C B R E U U C E C C I
Y U Y I A A F S Z I R H I Y Z
G H G T R H T M S T E S N E T
C S E N S I T I V E X F A E S
I I L A I V O J R G D Y M U O
M G B M R E P Y H R G L O X P
P G R O U C H Y C E I L M R Q
B U V R S E X Y K N A R C P T
S L L P D S O M B E R W U T E
X S V M J S E X J P W R K X O
```

BABY BOOM Page 102

```
Y P X R U U C T E E T H I N G
C I O J W A B E Y J T U S Y C
A F W F R S L A S K Q R P R H
C C E S O D B Y B Z E A I E M
K R E L A R D O C Y U S T S C
S A Y R T I M R N C F H U R C
T T C I A T A U E N K O P U A
B G R P N W O R L K E Q O N R
S L E O L G E B C A F T I D R
E R A I L A P A C I F I E R I
I G N N L L S S L O O R D B A
T G V A K K E W H P R U B I G
O I V Z O E H R M T J T Q R E
O Y J U D Z T N Z E A G U C K
B B L B S E L T T A R B Y Z Y
```

CUPPA JOE LINGO Page 103

```
B T S N Q A L B H W T Q R Z C
N E S E G M A C C H I A T O L
A T I N A R G K O C X C L Y W
U Y E P I U A K A D O U N L S
K X T S E Z L N G H M M U L S
U A T K C S N A D B V U D S E
F A A I A A S E I E X N E H R
J Q L N P M G A N T I L C Z P
M O Y N P E N T T M P E A C H
O O O Y U R I E O I L A F B C
D C S N C I W C H N M D L J N
R Y I O I C H W O V V E F P E
H J J T N A T C L Y H D D D Y
H D R F O N I C C U P P A R F
D O P P I O W O S S E R P S E
```

Word Searches

EARTH BELOW US Page 104

```
T T T H O K S T N K O F V Y K
N L E U F R D T H N C U K H J
Y E S L A E B O G F O R C E E
P G R M E N U I O L L O P A D
E R E H P S O M T A U C M X H
D A V H T A C R N N M K I N V
I V I O F C L O T O B E I S H
R I N R F F L D P S I T Z N X
Y T U H H U O V R E A S Y P N
L Y J Z C W F T J I N H S Z T
L M V K N W U V F H N U L I E
A I L F U F W J S I E T J T M
S Q B C A B G P O N L T B K B
A R S Z L Y G T B V G L V T J
N B K U M R L O H K R E V O R
```

GOLD RUSH Page 105

```
X S M I R N V H H B Y M L A U
D K T D W L C S G S I E Y E M
P V W A F A M W F N S A A E Z
F O H L T R E V E I R T E R S
E P N A W E T S G O O S E O S
T G S D W E W Z D C C Y K J D
V G C E L N T A I G Q P Y P I
O M E M B E R N R I B R I C K
I X F Q N O R U B R A E C B B
V P W Z L C L G E L I C R N Q
Y T E O A E V G T S A O C M V
S V C I C Y N E A O A R R B N
H K R V J I C T G P O D A S L
S Y K H F E P V T X K T E F Y
N R S Q H I M X Z M W G H Z U
```

209

TAKE ME OUT TO THE BALLGAME Page 106

```
B W N S I N G L E Z S U G U V
H A Y X P N P R G C X V J U S
O L S P F K W R A E P C R B H
J K T E V I R D E N I L B D M
E U R R S J O S R T D L R Z W
T J I F I L I U Q E T S R R O
N P K E O P O L T R H I L Z K
W O E C H U L A P F N C H A Z
K T X T O M L E D I I S T O M
U S T G M P A T P E T E X A N
W T C A E I B S T L D C L W C
J R M M R R Y Z F D A C H D E
V O O E U E L B U O D Y U E L
E H N W N F F A Q W S Z C T R
V S H U T O U T U O G U D U A
```

FRANKS AND BEANS Page 107

```
K O X G X Z X N Q D Q I O R E
P E I T B P M X K L H T U Y E
U K O E X Z V U M U C O N E X
P I N T O W S F N C L Q W T X
K D L F C D L L S I C U Y A U
X N I T G A R B A N Z O A D O
M E O G N I R T S N N A U B I
I Y L L O Y D W R I G H T R P
A F A V A R E E F H N E M N T
H Q Z W O V K Y I S V A L L I
L X N F N S A X J R V D T L R
E E F F O C B A V O F N H R A
F I O V M Y M W P G R E E N A
G L P B Y I Q A W B C M R T L
J J E L L Y G H T W I I H B H
```

Word Searches

WINE AND CHEESE, PLEASE! Page 108

```
W A J D W J O F P F O L O W H
P I N O T N O I R S H G T H J
Z H M A E R C G S I H T F H H
V M O I C O O T O L R E M Z X
Y G F Q T I N P Z B T H R M C
V T N T E N R E B A C S U R B
O G A I S A A E M H R S T S Y
E G R L L X D I M C C I B I V
E D F S L S D U H A N W H F H
Z W B Z R F E X T C R S P S X
B O Z U D N H I T V A S V Y X
Q J K X S R C H R K U D A B P
W W U T I I J W E B V F U L H
K A E Y K O I S I L O D V O A
A R B O W R Z Y R M N U P C G
```

DANCING DOWN MEMORY LANE Page 109

```
H C D J B W Q O H F G F V B P
G C O N G A S K G A P V E H Z
D T S I W T H N Y O L L T O H
G C T S C U F M H O E I T K U
J E R K W S M Y C C B A N E L
T P O P P I N O T B T U A Y L
I F L H H N M R A O A K M P Y
G K L S U O I R P N O J G O G
C E J B T C R D E Y P B N K U
M Z X I S E E R G L E O I E L
O U O L G H A D A G T K N Y L
W N I O S C I Q B X P S N Y Y
R D R A A A D A B M A L U O P
E X M M O O N W A L K X R H M
E C N A D N E K C I H C O I G
```

2 X 4 Page 110

```
D Z Y B H V D X F G X I Z O N
Y L I E W T Q U S Q A T T Y X
O I E W E N W E U B G R G Z Y
R V O E H P I L U T O J M W W
P L F K D R U T O U C A N U T
L K T R L U A O A B Y L N O K
M X A P J T N T U E S D A Y
J X E A W H N I H L L F F T O
M B Z E P N O G T A O O O O W
Z R L A A T H H M R C M R D R
S W S D L X R T T F O R M A L
T T E B R N G I E R O F U Y H
E N U T R O F O R G E O L A S
H K V V U Y F O R T Y R A G J
Y O V N C V W O Y S H K D V X
```

THE CAT'S OUT OF THE BAG Page 111

```
I L Z M J Y X B S U H I Q D P
P I Q A A H G I X N Q M B Q A
K I C N G I B L L O O K U D N
L Z O X N M N H C M P T R H T
O I U O H A T E E H C A M D H
L A G X I L I E C O P B E D E
E R A S N A A R A O B B S S R
M R R Y Y Y R C E W O Y E D C
Z E O D H A L L A B I N M Q T
P G G C U N L X T R I G A Z B
T I N G I O O A D L A S I Q B
J T A C D L I W A W J C S C M
W J J G Y L A B F B R L F S N
D Z A M U P B C L T M G T E Y
I R H H R M R P T M X D E E E
```

210

Word Searches

LOVE IS IN THE AIR Page 112

```
T S F L Q H V G I L O S T I N
P Y M Y F I T S U J A P H R Z
M E M I T S E K A T O U E E G
D W G D C R A Z Y Y C V R D W
A N V R A N W A P N P R E N B
G I I Y O H F P L I W K I E P
Y N S R O O U C G L E O S T O
C O I E E P V O H L O T N E W
J Q O N A G T Y Y A O U E M E
U J N D R O A L K F P R T N R
F O O L D U F N M I I E Y O O
F I F E B A B Y E N N M L O F
P I P S K N I T S E X D M O F
W F O S G N I W E H T N O I F
C R U O Y O D O H W L A M F N
```

LAND DOWN UNDER Page 113

```
N U Z K V F Y S U P Y T A L P
D U B A R B I E Z B L O K E K
O C L O A T D N J K O A L A Y
E H Y L V P I I M K N I G E G
Y M L E A G T G Z G D A Y D J
X A E U R R K I A O W O Y I G
W A N C I O B R C O P P W N G
M G X A K B O O M E R A N G S
M C C L C O R B R H D L E O E
H N S Y A C A A A P H S N E T
B J R P B T H G L R L L D S W
Q Y A T T O O C I D N A B O E
L V C U U Y I V E G E M I T E
S H X S O P B H H O W I A N Q
S P E P M I R H S U B M Z Z Y
```

RIGHT AS RAIN Page 114

```
F S U C C R I O R R L D P F O
Y I P L F Z J V B H M L F V Y
D P W O B N I A R D P H N T K
D F N D R I Z Z L E A K T C H
V O L T W D V Z G L K G J P R
F R Q Y B I S B I U E C U Z E
F E L D D U P G J G X R I X N
C S L O O A H E C E P E B L K
J T C K W T F H R L X D J M S
G O P B N D B L E S O N J E U
S O O I P I I C W Z Y U Q B S
H B N A O G R Y O H O H D Z R
N G C J U R X P H A E T X A T
Y I H M R O T S S I T S J T J
D D O O L F D U S L G N N N Q
```

DO YOU BELIEVE IN MAGIC? Page 115

```
S X S J R J Y S F E P O R U S
E D M I L H H G E S K G A H E
K X R H V S C O C V D N A W V
T S W A O T R B U T O H Y D O
S H S R C C U O I D Q L L E D
C G E W A R U G R U I E G N S
A N P C T E E S E R I N S O A
R I T O O R P R P F I M I T L
F N N A S U A P R O O M P S N
N N C A H B N E A K C T Q K I
F E A A B P P T E S S U J C L
Y H N I P P O Z P I I B S A R
O V T A O E T T Q F N D U L E
R Z N C D E I R F G E I S B M
C H D A B H A S S L E E V E T
```

Word Searches

MONSTER MASH Page 116

```
C R C T H I A U W T Q G V Y Z
H S F S W A M P T H I N G N J
S Y R R M U M M Y D D E R F K
T K A E A N Z R Z R B F E W G
U E N T Y N U H M L I N M E G
E R K S D M V Y Q A G C L L O
C H E N Y U L D N V F M I V D
A S N U T A R E F S O N N Z Z
S D S M I K E W A Z O W S K I
U H T E C A F R E H T A E L L
D A E H N I P A L U C A R D L
E J I T H H F C H C N I R G A
M N N M D A C A T P P C M L E
Q V W E I K O O C G R O V E R
J A S O N A M F L O W S V R D
```

LOST AND CROWNED Page 117

```
Q L S D I N S P A C E A Y B Q
M U O E B F E R G I E E A A U
K I E R L C C A U S E S D F E
I D S E T R O S G L Y T I F E
N N D S N N A O I N T A R O N
G I C S U E O H P V O O F H L
R M I I Y N L C C E L K G Y A
I R B D N E I I E E R E N M T
C U O O Y A K V Z T C L I M I
H O Y W C D T R E A O N K I F
A Y S N I I A I A R B M I J A
R P R I N C E L T C S E E R H
D L I A G A E R D N A E T R P
K I N G A R T H U R N E C H J
E A M E L I A E A R H A R T F
```

AMERICAN IDLE Page 118

```
X N L O C N I L Q U S A M M
R I A V R O C D N Q P G O U
V C Q F A I R L A N E D N S
K J A S E I T V Q D E R Z T
A E L L B P D S E L D I A A
O Y P E L E U N T T S B N N
H A R J S I E O L E T R T G
N I D O E A D V C R E E W Q
F S T U D E B A K E R D H I
F O R O C L P R C D C N P T
V O N I M A C L E E A U W Y
V S T I N G R A Y V M H E A
T C H A R G E R H L A T Y D
I C R I M P A L A E R B G B
Z W T E L R R B T B O B K I
```

WHAT ABOUT BOB? Page 119

```
V M Q N G O L D T H W A I T F
D Y B Z P R L Q O W C U H X T
M S R Z Y R S P O N G E B O B
M K N V N J E H A S B U Y Y K
W X R U T R S L I U F B H W U
C S M V J E I L I F S A G E T
C U O V D V E L A R W N C O G
W O G I N N D L B A R K E R F
T Q S N T E O E K E E S J R M
H Z A T R D L D D R Z B W O N
J D S O A Z P Y M H E D O Y F
Q Y O N H S B R O W N G Q J K
X L D L W V L N M O J N E P W
M A R L E Y Z C E R F H U S K
I N F D N Q K I R V D K F I C
```

• Armchair Puzzlers • Solutions •

Word Searches

LAW AND ORDER Page 120

```
C B S W B S P R I X C Y G U S
A E H V Q D L N O B G N S P Z
X R O T C A Z H U B I O D U T
L J R D G O E T C R B L I J K
W R R E S I U R C P L E A U H
X R L A S S J R D R W F R R U
U L N T L T E S T I M O N Y O
I O I Y U G S F E D S U A I J
E N G A D Y R F N N C T P S Y
G T S U B S R U D O T J L I Q
K R J J S O C C B O C E N P S
U J U A T C I D R E V U N X L
J C T K S S E N T I W F V C C
M I S D E M E A N O R G X T E
M I O X W Y S H E Y V U Y A N
```

TOYS OF SUMMER Page 121

```
L T S M G N A B B E F N U E S
I C A L O R I Q E T U Q S O P
A S I O I G A B Z G A R E R R
K F D L W P S D T S O O E D I
P L L H B I N R I H E K L S N
E O E E R K I S G O A T B F K
G E O F V U F N L O F M I L L
L X T H Q O I O S I O L I K E
S O E S A R H R G B D A Y D R
N B S F P L E S R Q P E D E X
O D G S I P U E W A S E E S R
R N Q U W T H G O G G L E S S
K A I S G A J U N G L E G Y M
E S W U W S E O H S E S R O H
L Y S F L I P P E R S C T Y K
```

SILVER SCREEN Page 122

```
D Z Y C I T Y L I G H T S Y G
O G R A L Y E K B E N H U R O
V O O C F T E G H P K B N O X
J L T S D R I B E H T D S T A
O D S L C G I R S H A N E S W
L Y E R I O H C Y S P N T E F
G E V E T U O B A L L A B D O
N L O G I T R E V N R I L I E
O L L B Z V F E A I Q U V S S
K E P B E T I Y S J I U D T U
G R A C N A L B A S A C E S O
N V B A K N O O N H G I H E H
I W I Z A R D O F O Z F C W N
K G M D N U O B L L E P S A L
E T A K E M S S I K C U D R A
```

SLANG TIME Page 123

```
V S H I D H A D C R J X C M A
W H Y M I B M V X I W T J P V
P Z G C A W R U D A Z W W L W
G W G B W T H E I L I I Z D Y
O N I L L A B A K W D B C Q K
G R J H L I S G C S Y Q Z C O
C Q F F C F N S H K R N A B A
G Q K E M I I G U Y E M O H B
R A S Q S G K M B P L D S L G
O B Y S P P Z X O L L O I T P
F U O H H L N D U U I W J R W
J L D O A O A B N B H N K I F
F G U R T V E Y C L C L G P P
W J D T D Y V I E F R O N T E
M O E Y S B M B K R S W E E T
```

· Armchair Puzzlers · Solutions ·

Word Searches

AMERICA THE BEAUTIFUL Page 124

```
S K R A Z O G S D O O W D E R
L L E B Y T R E B I L Y D A L
T G N S E D A L G R E V E N E
E E O I T S N E S E H R B E I
U T T E A X D M A O O U U L P
E T S T G G C P L H O S N D P
S Y W I N L A I T A V H K E I
U S O M E Y N R L T E M E E S
O B L E D S Y E A D R O R N S
H U L S L I O S K F D R H E I
E R E O O K N T E E A E I C S
T G Y Y G A L A M O M L L A S
I R K C O R H T U O M Y L P I
H C R A Y A W E T A G S B S M
W D S E A R S T O W E R C T N
```

DOUBLE Ds Page 125

```
A Q M U G C V R T G I M Q H M
F B Y E Z W Z T C W J R Q S N
Y P S E S A J C A O E U L F C
E O H V E Q T O D D Y Y R M R
T L U N N D E T D A T S W F E
M P D S T Y O A Y I S N Y F G
F C D D D C E L D D U C K Y W S
J R E V I T I D D A J Q B W N
Y Z R L D F O R U B S W P D W
Y P T O D D L E R Y A E T A C
S A A F A D L S C E D L D X N
B L M D D D I S P U D D L E Y
K T X D D C M W R P L D U C C
H P E I Y L U E T E E I U M C
P M M E T V E C W L G R G R O
```

MOVIE MUNCHIES Page 126

```
H O T D O G Y F G A K B U S R
G J W M I L K D U D S O Q E A
Q K I L C U H P M B P E T L I
Y A Z J H A O E M M A P A T S
Y Y Z A U P S E Y N C Y K T I
V S L D C N U C B W O K T I N
N W E O K M I K E A N D I K E
J Q R S L M Q O A F S C K S T
U N S R E K A E R B W A J G T
J A R E S E D W S M R Y L N E
U C E P T S R E K C I N S J S
B H B P O W S S N O B N O B Q
E O O O D S E L A M A T T O H
S S O H Y D D A D R A G U S F
C E G W P X N N N F M P S M T
```

GOING TO THE CHAPEL Page 127

```
I D M D E N H H K B M R M Q M
D B J N O O M Y E N O H R K C
S B F I R S T D A N C E U X B
R V N M D I A M O N D R Z V A
X U M A N H S H Y W I Q M H L
K S P R P T F A Q O B D C B B
L N E F L O W E R G I R L R Z
T T O Q D A L I M A U I R P F
E E N I E S Y I M H T U V J K
U X A X I T N S C O R L E D V
Q M M A R I E W A E I G A O U
U Q T W S D L A K A N S W C M
O F S T I I F L E H G S O I E
B C E R E M O N Y D S G E W Q
O R B V Q C U I V J X P K N D
```

· Armchair Puzzlers · Solutions ·

Word Searches

RED-LETTER DAY Page 128

```
U F K R Q E B G Y G I O C C F
P Y C L V V B I S I M K W K E
M R U A O K A U A D J D V J Z
Y R R E B W A R T S F E Y E X
R E T S B O L S T T L D O Z E
F H E A D N G I S P O T S U N
D C R S E F D X P O E N E N X
D N I O O V K A H S T P S T S
L D F X F N T G O O T W P E A
F L X Z X V N P N L E I A E S
D K Z F H I A W D I V S C S R
O K H T D P R D O L R F O K O
A R L I A G D H X L O R I R C
J S R F U F Y P U H C T E K K
N R W B F T H G I L F P Z H S
```

LONG LIVE THE KING Page 129

```
A D N A L E C A R G M D H S J
L M S R X D G S R O J A S T A
L E D E F A P U O C W F U I I
I M R H Y I X R I A O E N U L
C P O T H H E S I T I W G S H
S H C O Q L G I C R A L L P O
I I E M G O O H A O L R A M U
R S R N S L O M I O K T S U S
P B U P E U A D R B C R S J E
K J E P N S U N M B D H E R R
O L U D I T K S L R I G S R O
R T D L S C S A G E V S A L C
F O X N O E D E U S E U L B K
G M U R L E N O L O C E H T I
V S A C C H A R I T Y K V R R
```

DOG-EAT-DOG Page 130

```
S S K L C K R T S P O O D L E
F N A D K E O N R E I K R O Y
G T H B T C M A L T E S E R D
J T N U R C C H I H U A H U A
C L S K Z E U K D G E T P O C
J S G N O L T O O F R U E M H
V K T E N A D T A E R G H R S
L N T B F G T D Y N T W S A H
M I O F E N W A Y F R A N K U
H L H R L R M S N A H T A N N
K T D W G R N K K A Y E M T D
U O E H A V B A L L P A R K O
G H R C E R E T R I E V E R B
R E S E B O X E R D V N G Y N
C O L L I E K A K M V Z E H G
```

SOUTH OF THE BORDER Page 131

```
B Q O O L R N Y N D A R K I R
U P L Y D Z S A E Y B O P K M
H H D K A U H A U H I H C C F
U C N C B M A R G A R I T A Z
D S O M B R E R O U X W C R T
R A H T A M S D I M A R Y P D
V S N I A T N U O M C U U O V
Z T N Y P Z O N S C C T A N Z
Y T A D E S E R T A N A S C Q
T R L M C P M V T W L I A H B
E P I N A T A A R I U S C O T
G D A L C L N O U E L Q A P C
Q S A A T P E Q G L C L R R L
H J R T U Y E S C E T Z A U A
Z H U V S T C H I L E C M K U
```

215

· Armchair Puzzlers · Solutions ·

Word Searches

GET LUCKY Page 132

```
Y D Y L B W B R E K O O N S E
K D M E O M A H J O N G C V T
V A M G N I C A R E S R O H I
C J U D O M C Q K Y A E B X S
N T R I M B A R W T H Y Q U W
M A O R M I R R C K R H D H S
G M U B A L A H D P E O D E L
N S L L G L T L O A M U H H O
B Y E A K I V W R I K N E N T
Z R T C C A E T N G S D I S S
Q E T K A R S O A O P S E U I
A T E J B D E G T W A D F C P
A T V A T S A N A C R E K O P
S O L C O S R I I R C E F J N
J L K K T V U B L T Z N M K L
```

SUIT YOURSELF Page 133

```
J A R Y Z G T L B Q B T U D M
Z K G G I P L N E S A D E M M
J K Z W D E R O L I A T N A S
G B C D S C D N H H S R F P W
B U Z O J E C H W A R U C O I
G S O A X I E T E B F L R K M
O J O U E P I R T S N I P E R
V G T C P E B T S A I L O R W
K N N W A E C N I U C B W B B
D I Z I L R B L K N C D Z Q P
W G P B H H A S O S H K Q A C
C G U O F T W W P W H Z E X Z
D O B D I N A M R A N H N R P
D J K Y H E U B E L C F N I T
N F Y F I J F Q E G V E O A Q
```

WHAT A GOOD SPORT! Page 134

```
C R Y S F L O G N I T A K S R
W R E S T L I N G R Q V O Q T
Z G I R E C C O S N W U T U B
E H O C K E Y P R D I S T A V
S X B V K J B G A S V H H S Z
W N R A N E T N C E O B S H F
S T N B S Z T I Q S L S B I F
W F U O A K T P U S L O A O F
I P X X J S E C E O E F O L V
M R K I A A E T T R Y T R O C
M L G N F B V B B C B B K P Z
I L M G Z A M E A A A A C T D
N Y R E H C R A L L L L A N F
G D B I G S U L L I L L R E A
P G O P V Q Z S I N N E T F W
```

• Armchair Puzzlers • Solutions •